THE FEMININE
CRISIS IN
CHRISTIAN FAITH

THE FEMININE CRISIS IN CHRISTIAN FAITH

ELIZABETH ACHTEMEIER

ABINGDON PRESS

NEW YORK   NASHVILLE

THE FEMININE CRISIS IN CHRISTIAN FAITH

Copyright © 1965 by Abingdon Press

All rights in this book are reserved.
No part of the book may be reproduced in any manner whatsoever without written permission of the
publishers except brief quotations embodied in criti-
cal articles or reviews. For information address
Abingdon Press, Nashville, Tennessee.

Library of Congress Catalog Card Number: 65-20366

Scripture quotations unless otherwise noted are from the
Revised Standard Version of the Bible, copyrighted 1946
and 1952 by the Division of Christian Education, National Council of Churches, and are used by permission.

SET UP, PRINTED, AND BOUND BY THE
PARTHENON PRESS, AT NASHVILLE,
TENNESSEE, UNITED STATES OF AMERICA

IN GRATITUDE

to God for my family—
my husband Paul
our son Mark
and our little girl Marie

CONTENTS

CONTENTS

CHAPTER I
A STILL MORE EXCELLENT WAY

Frankly, I admire my fellow American women. I admire them for their accomplishments. In a society which has perpetuated the myth of their inability to drive a car safely or to construct an argument logically, they have gradually but steadily won for themselves a place of increasing influence and respect.

Women gained the vote in the United States only in 1920, but since that time they have become important participants in both political parties. Their views are carefully assessed and cultivated by every political candidate. In the last century, few married women had any money of their own. Women now control a large share of the wealth in this wealthiest country of the world. Their buying habits occupy the attention of many of the nation's advertisers. Though often told that their "place is in the home," American women nevertheless now make up an indispensable part of the nation's labor force. Six out of every ten women in the country are employed outside of their homes. Increasing educational opportunities have led American women into practically every occupation known to men. Though executive positions and equal pay are still largely denied to women, few employers are ignorant of the contributions females make to the general welfare. "Womanpower" is now a fact to be reckoned with in the political, economic, and business life of the United States.

Nor is the American female any less accomplished in the realm of her home. She may rely heavily on precooked and packaged foods, but she is still among the world's best cooks, and she lays her table with an imagination and knowledge of nutrition second to that of few others. She usually buys her clothes ready-made from the store, but she selects her dress with a taste which has led designers to call her "the best-dressed woman in the world." She is not a slavish housekeeper, and she washes, irons, and dusts only because she has to, but nevertheless, the art of "homemaking" occupies much of her thought and energy. The women I know can entertain with a polish. They are concerned with interior decorating. They often garden or sew or do handiwork to add to the beauty of their houses. Their principal interest in life is the welfare of their husbands and children, and they will make almost any sacrifice to see that their families get ahead. They are constantly studying and experimenting to make themselves better wives and mothers.

Added to these accomplishments must be the achievements of these women in their local communities, for women are active throughout the country in every area of civic and social life. It is they who often staff our innumerable voluntary social service agencies—the Red Cross, the League of Women Voters, the YWCA, the Scouts, the community recreational and service centers. On any given day in the United States women can be found giving speeches, running bazaars, serving benefit teas, sewing at hospitals, collecting used clothing, serving hot lunches to the under-privileged, visiting the sick, guiding youth groups, chauffering or talking or planning or collecting for one good cause after another. The general picture is one of responsible females, freely and actively engaged in furthering the prosperity and welfare of all. It can truly be said that in the United States, women have "come of age" and have taken their place in our society as mature and responsible participants. When I look at the accomplishments of all the women I know, I cannot help but find them admirable.

In the light of these admittedly generalized facts, I would therefore like to raise some specific questions: Has the American female equally come of age religiously? Does she know as much about her Christian faith as she does about running her household? Has she expressed her faith as adequately as she has her commitment to her family and community? Has the American female, in short, accomplished as much in the theological realm?

Certainly, on the face of it, the answer to these questions must be yes. For if we consider just those women in the church, their contributions to their faith have been invaluable. Perhaps it has has been in the realm of missions that their record has been most noteworthy. Let us look very briefly at the history of their activities.[1]

As early as the beginning of the nineteenth century women formed into local groups in communities throughout this country for the purpose of studying and supporting foreign missions. The "Female Mite Society," the "Pious Female Praying Society," the "Cent Society"—such were the names of their organizations, and

[1] I am indebted for much of the following history to an account of the United Church Women: *Follow Those Women* by Gladys Gilkey Calkins (New York: National Council of the Churches of Christ in the U.S.A., 1961).

11

their monetary contributions came from butter and egg money, from selling baked goods, from piecing quilts and sewing rags into carpets. But that which began on a small scale swelled into a mighty flood of personnel and goods and dollars. The first women missionaries went abroad in the 1860's. The Nationwide Day of Prayer for Foreign Missions began in 1890. By 1900 American women had begun to print mission literature for study at home. By 1914 they were sending Christian literature for women and children abroad to mission outposts. In the 1920's they took up support of Christian colleges in other lands. In the decades that followed they brought innumerable Christians from other countries to speak and study in the United States.

The significance of such interest in the missionary outreach of the church goes far beyond any immediate results in terms of numbers of heathen converted, however. Women's mission study and support laid the basis in the United States for much that was to follow. Before the ecumenical movement was ever known in this country, women were finding in their missionary endeavors common bases for cooperative work on the local level. As early as 1887 there were "Missionary Unions," "Missionary Federations," "Councils of Missions" in various cities, where women of all denominations had banded together in a common zeal to evangelize the world.

It was this zeal and their sense of the oneness of the church in its mission, which caused American women not only to declare their unity with Christians in Germany in the dark days of 1939, but which also led them to offer the first hands of friendship to the Axis nations after World War II. Because women had studied their missionary literature, they had an international concern. That concern expressed itself in every possible way, from work with Japanese-Americans in relocation camps during World War II, to the shipment, in 1945, of one million diapers overseas. It led a

12

million and a half United States women to sign cards in 1948, promising to support the United Nations. It led the United Church Women to take up, in 1957, a study of emerging nations. There can be no doubt that much of the female support for this country's role as a responsible international leader found its seedbed first of all in the monthly missionary sewing circle, gathered in the parlor of the neighborhood church to chat, but also to learn.

Though mission work has been perhaps the principal interest of the American church woman, it certainly has not been the only one. Women have also made lasting contributions to the social outreach of the church. Immediately after the Civil War, a few women's groups braved scorn and criticism by starting humanitarian projects in various communities to aid the poor or the females working in new factories. In the first decades of the twentieth century, women took a helping interest in the plight of the immigrants crowding through Ellis Island. And they firmly insisted, against the economic reasoning of their husbands, that industrial workers should be protected by legislation and the right to organize. As early as 1920 the needs of the sharecroppers and migrants had come to church women's attention. It was first of all their interest in these itinerant workers which led the church as a whole to set up a comprehensive ministry to migrants after the Second World War. Again, it was women's home mission groups which gave some of the first aid to the American Indian, just as it was the same female organizations which, as early as 1926, began nationwide studies of race relations.

In fact, women's church groups have a notable record in support of Negro rights. Not only have they long practiced integration in their national organizations, such as the YWCA or the United Church Women, but their statements against the evils of segregation were some of the strongest made in the 1940's. After the Supreme Court decision of 1954 they set up local and regional workshops to help communities in the transition from segregation to integration. In recent years, many of them have continued local and nation-wide support of the civil rights movement.

In 1953 against the trend in much of the rest of the country, swept by "McCarthyism," the United Church Women also had the courage to issue a study guide on "Loyalty and Freedom," attempting to distinguish between the Christian approach to social issues and communist theory and practice. Indeed, as early as 1926 church women were studying, on a nation-wide basis, subjects as significant as "law observance," "Christian citizenship," "industrial and race relations," "international relations and world peace." In the past two decades, they have branched out into everything from "ecumenical world tours" to leadership training programs in local communities.

There is no doubt that women's place in the church in America has been as active and indispensable participants. Often without official authority, usually apart from policymaking bodies of the church, women have nevertheless managed to make their voices and consciences heard in the land. Their record of accomplishments in the realm of religion has been remarkable indeed.

Yet despite these unmistakable achievements in the service of our faith, we American women have sometimes crippled our efforts to serve our Lord. For one thing, we sometimes have approached our tasks with a certain naïveté, which has impressed our society as rather amusing and typical of our efforts.

For example, if we look once more at the history of our achievements, we find that we have sometimes had the naïve tendency to "think big." In the 1930's we women decided to improve motion pictures. And so, with little thought of the complex moral problems involved, 400,000 of us on the East coast set out to approve or boycott the currently-showing products of Hollywood. Needless to say, we do the same thing today whenever we mothers start banding together for a moral America. To cite another example, in 1936 the

14

National Council of Federated Church Women held what they considered to be a highly successful conference in Dayton, Ohio. But the theme of this conference was, amazingly, "Exploring and Possessing the Unclaimed Areas of Life in Citizenship, Personal Living, World Peace, and Economics." It was an all-embracing theme, quite typical of our women's conferences. But in such all-embracing generality we have tended to give secular society the impression that we have naïvely bitten off more than we can chew. Our efforts on behalf of our faith seem to have been marked by a certain unaware simplicity at times. And this simplicity has made us more the objects of amusement than of interest in our cause.

At other times, however, we have not amused our secular society. We have angered and repelled it. And very often we have done so quite unintentionally. I think it is true to say that most American church women are dedicated to the Lord they serve. They are sincerely interested in applying their Christian faith to their daily practice. And yet, in such dedication and zeal for our faith, we sometimes offend the very souls we would attract. Consider the following poem, written by one of our number:

> It is coming! Hark, the sound is on the air!
>   It rolls like thunderous waves across a sea—
> The tramp of millions drawn from everywhere
>   In the great advance of Christianity.
> They come, these followers of the living Christ,
>   Marching with their lifted flags unfurled;
> They bring a gift that never could be priced
>   To a hurt, bewildered, and chaotic world—
> A world whose chaos man himself has wrought,
>   A world that flounders in its dark despair.
> They offer that which lands have ever sought
>   And failed to find unless the Christ be there.
> And now they come, these great onrushing throngs,

15

> Aflame with God, with a will that does not cease,
> To bring salvation and to right the wrongs
> Of all the world in desperate need of peace.[2]

Irrespective of its literary merits, when we church women read this poem, we often find it inspirational, a fitting expression of the determination and zeal which we have for the cause of Christ. But when a woman outside of the church reads such poems, she is likely to see in them something else. She is likely to see in them self-righteousness—the claim that we Christian women are on the side of right and salvation, and that we alone, therefore, are able to save the world. Such a claim does not accord very well with the biblical proclamation of the unrighteousness of all men. As a result, the person outside of the church is rightly repelled by such a claim and reacts to such a message in scorn or bitterness. We sometimes express our faith, it seems, inadequately and without self-examination.

Indeed, if we Christian women will take a close look at ourselves, it may become clear that we not only sometimes inadequately express our faith, but that many of us are also rather confused as to just exactly what the content of our Christian faith is. Consider the activities which go on in local church women's groups throughout the country. Many of these activities are worthwhile and soundly Christian, to be sure. But many more of them are in direct contradiction to Christian devotion and belief.

For example, I have been in groups in which the women, quite unaware, were involved in the baldest kind of natural religion. Not too long ago, I listened to a female retreat leader: "As I look at these lovely trees and the wonderful grass here in this park," she exuded, "I know from all of this beauty that God is with us." The

---

[2] From *Meditations* by Grace Noll Crowell. Copyright 1951 by Pierce and Smith (Abingdon Press).

16

beauty of the natural world was for her the pledge of God's presence. But what, then, is the meaning of the risen Christ's *promise* to be with us, and why was it necessary that our Lord give that promise? There is some confusion here as to the basis of Christian certainty. Yet women engaged in such natural religion will fill their worship services with poems about nature's revelations and wonders. Occasionally, as with the group I attended, they will depart to a rustic spot for "retreat and renewal," on the unspoken assumption that a return to nature is at the same time a return to God. They have not grasped the fact that the Christian God is revealed, not in nature, but in a history.

I have also known groups of Christian women who seemed lost in an uncritical humanism. They talked of the "divine spark" within them. They made themselves the measure of all truth, accepting only what they liked. And they planned their programs on the presupposition that sooner or later they could bring in the kingdom of God. They seemed never to have become aware of the real meaning of the Christian witness to the sovereignty of God or of the Christian confession of the sinfulness of all men.

Again, I have been among groups of Christian women who were dedicated to finding "oneness" with God, and their search for mystical union with their Lord led them into all sorts of experiments. Some women I know will uncritically accept Hindu or other forms of oriental mysticism. But they seem to have no awareness of the fact that such non-Christian mystical faiths, in their neglect of history, are at complete odds with the Christian revelation. There is here evidenced a basic misunderstanding of the nature of the biblical faith.

This same inability to distinguish the Christian from the non-Christian is evidenced, too, in the kind of religious interpretations we women accept, indeed by the kind of witness to God for which we women often pay our money. Hollywood has put out numerous "biblical spectaculars," and I will readily admit that sometimes such films are entertaining. I recall that a reviewer termed one of them a "biblical *Gone with the Wind*." One can legitimately enjoy a wide-screen splash of technicolor. But nevertheless, it must be admitted that most such spectaculars are banal distortions of the message of the Bible. Yet the surprising fact is that I have heard women praise such films as fine Christian witnesses, simply because the films ostensibly dealt with Jesus or David or a similar figure. There seems to be here an ignorance of the actual content of the Christian proclamation.

Along the same line, it is instructive to examine the religious novels we women read. Again, they can be enjoyed for their entertainment value. But when such books are sentimental fabrications of biblical fact, completely distorting the Bible's realism and profundity, we surely must question if these books are "inspirational" as I have heard women say they are. Do they inspire in us faith in the *biblical* God, and do they add in any way to our knowledge of Christianity? They convey a certain religious message, to be sure, but very often that message has little to do with the Christian proclamation.

The fact is that we women sometimes uncritically accept anything with a religious label, because we do not have the knowledge necessary to separate the Christian from the non-Christian. It is no accident that each political campaign brings forth candidates in this country who indiscriminately appeal to God and the Bible as the supporters of their programs or who claim that righteousness and morality are on their side alone. The politicians know that in the minds of many, "religion," no matter how distorted, is considered "good." And it is to this stereotype of religion as good that the candidate makes his appeal. The disturbing fact is that the appeal goes over with many of our women, simply because we are not sure enough of our own religious position to sort out fact from fiction. We must therefore uncritically accept almost any religious offering.

In short, we women are not adequately versed in Christian theology. We are not certain enough about just what we believe and why it is we believe it. We are not sure enough of the distinctively Christian witness to God. We may have accomplished wonders in our homes, our communities, and our churches. But far too few of us have mastered the basic essentials of the Christian faith.

When we get into discussion groups or panel debates, we sometimes become aware of our theological inadequacies. We find that we do not know just why God considers us sinful. Or we have a hard time explaining clearly what it is that Jesus Christ has done. Or we admit that we have never thought very much about the goal of God's activity in the world. Or we find ourselves hard put to define just what the church is and what it is called to do.

Sometimes, when we have gaps in our knowledge and understanding of our faith, we tend to fill them in with the products of our own wishful thinking. Especially does this seem to be true of our beliefs about life after death. I have encountered among church women everything from a nonbiblical belief in the automatic immortality of all souls to a conviction that heaven is the place where we continue to work toward our own perfection.

This is not to say that we women do not accept the Christian gospel when it is presented to us. As good members of the church we thank the minister at the sanctuary door each Sunday for his fine scriptural message. But then many of us construct our own personal beliefs in direct contradiction to that message, unaware that we are harboring within ourselves irreconcilable theological positions. It is not that we women reject the Christian witness to God. Our trouble is that many of us are not theologically learned enough to distinguish the Christian from the non-Christian.

Now theology is the attempt to deal in an orderly fashion with

19

our knowledge of God. And certainly our feminine inadequacies in theology are not due to an inability to organize. The daily schedule of the middle-class American woman is frequently a model of organization, and European housewives are often aghast at the range of activities their sisters in America can cover with apparent ease. Nor is the American woman's inadequacy as a theologian due to her lack of intelligence. American females can, and do, master everything from Dr. Spock to the history of French impressionism. An orderly understanding of the prophets or of the Gospel according to Mark does not seem an insurmountable intellectual barrier. No, our inadequacies in understanding our faith stem very often from our lack of awareness of our own shortcomings or from our neglect to seek for correction and growth.

In all fairness, let me say, however, that it is not we women alone who are at fault on this score. Our men in the churches could be shown to be equally theologically inadequate. I am analyzing the religious knowledge of women simply because I happen to be one of them, and because I may be able, therefore, to understand their problems from the inside out. I think I have experienced, either for myself or in the lives of loved ones, every religious error that is mentioned in this book. Therefore, I hope only to share the results of my own pilgrimage. At the same time, as part of my own confession, let me say that the preachers and teachers of the church, of whom I now am one, must accept a large part of the responsibility for the theological inadequacies of both men and women. Too often we have failed to make the Christian proclamation clear!

In response to all of this, perhaps some women will say that I am making a mountain out of a molehill. Is theology, after all, so important in women's lives? Does it matter very much that we do not know exactly what we believe? What's the difference if we praise the wrong movies or books or believe a political candidate or experiment with non-Christian worship practices and positions? Do these things really do any harm in our lives? After all, we women have a magnificent record of achievement in the church. We have accomplished amazing results in American society. Is not what we do much more important than what we believe or disbelieve?

This attitude is reflected to a certain extent in the history of female activities. Consider the following quotation from our history of the United Church Women: "The battle of Fundamentalism versus Liberalism [in the 1920's] might rage in the pulpits, and the Scopes trial make headlines in the newspapers, but these would not throw the women off course. There was too much that needed to be done." [3] The point here is not that this quotation reflects only the attitude of church women in the 1920's. The point is that it reflects also the attitude of its author in 1961. She herself—I am sure without meaning to do so—sees the 1920 battle over the basic authority of the Christian faith to be irrelevant to women's practice of that faith in society. Theology has taken a place second to that of activity.

It must be pointed out, however, that each of us is some kind of theologian. Each of us approaches life and its decisions on the basis of some kind of knowledge of God. If that knowledge is confused and contradictory and distorted, we will act on the basis of such confusion and contradiction and distortion. But if our knowledge is ordered and sound and well-founded, our activities can reflect the same qualities.

By way of example, let me tell you about three women I know of in the church. In a past issue of our denominational journal one of these women wrote an article after the death of her son. She ecstatically informed us that she had made "spirit contacts" with her son through the instrument of a medium, and she declared that these contacts had now given her "proof" of the resurrection of Christ. Despite the approving reader response which this woman

[3] Calkins, *Follow Those Women*, p. 19.

21

received, her article was a pitiful contrast to the certainty of the Christian church, which eternally is called to praise and proclaim the victory of a risen Lord. But this woman was acting and witnessing on the basis of her theology.

Another woman of my acquaintance holds the belief that God has established "spiritual laws" in the universe, and that eventually we will discover these, enabling us to live in peace and joy. It is as if God's work is done in the world and the living Christ has no function. The introduction of the kingdom of God awaits only an advance in man's knowledge. And so this woman's hope for the future is framed in terms of this belief. What happens to such a hope in the face of man's evil or lack of progress? The very happiness of this woman in the future rests on her theology.

A third good church woman sees certain moralistic rules as part and parcel of her faith, and anyone who breaks one of these rules cannot possibly be "religious" in her eyes. Thus she looks down on those who drink, for example, and she automatically cuts herself off from association with such souls. Therefore, she can never communicate the Gospel to anyone who imbibes, and she forms a striking contrast to her Lord, who made himself a friend of tax collectors and sinners, and who, because of his associations, bore the charge of being "a glutton and a drunkard" (Matt. 11:19; Luke 7:34).

The point is that each of these women lives and acts on the basis of her theology, and because the theology of each is inadequate, her own life reflects her confusion. In the same manner, our lives reflect the beliefs we hold, and if those beliefs are inadequate or distorted, our lives will bear their faulty stamp.

Certainly our own witness and work for Christ have sometimes borne the stamp of our theological inadequacy. Why is it that the term "missionary" has taken on a certain sense of scorn in our society? Is it because it has become synonymous with the interests of a well-meaning group of females, who sometimes cannot make clear themselves just why they are supporting missions? Or why is it that the "women's work" of the church holds a certain distasteful-ness for most male ministers? Is it because we women sometimes have little understanding of the theological position of our pastor, and that, therefore, he finds us impossible to reason with and un-changeable in our ways?

We women need to test ourselves with a question to find out just how theologically aware we are: How many of us can outline the theological position of our local pastor? For the fact is that our pastor has a theological position. He has particular beliefs about God, about man, about the nature of the world and of history. And our pastor has constructed his parish program on the basis of such beliefs. His leadership of worship, his recommendations for the educational program of the Sunday school, his relations with his people grow out of his theological understanding. But if we are unaware of his theological position, we cannot understand the reasons why he does what he does. Thus, we judge him all too often by superficials—by his mannerisms, his regularity in calling, his appearance of sincerity, the ease with which he gets along with the young people. Often many of us cannot understand, or we consider unimportant, the theological bases of his actions. Such fact has plunged many a young pastor, fresh out of seminary, into dis-illusionment and despair. One such young graduate, after two years of answering female critics, confessed that he had turned down the proffered presidency of a women's college because he found it impossible to *reason* with the women members of his con-gregation.

I think his complaint was justified to a certain extent. Many of us are really not adequately prepared to reason theologically. Therefore, in place of thought in our religion we substitute feeling. We seek not logical theological positions, but "mountaintop ex-periences." We act not on the basis of biblical convictions, but because something seems to do some good. Too often our criterion for good or bad is the question, "Is it spiritual?" And the spiritual is then accepted with a final subjective measurement, which for many of us is the yardstick of all religious truth: "I like it."

1.

We have yet really to answer the question as to whether or not theology is important in our lives, however. And perhaps I best can answer it by pointing out the present-day consequences of our theological inadequacies. It is these consequences which reveal the deeply tragic nature of our theological shortcomings, and it is the seriousness of these consequences which has led me to undertake this book.

In the first place, because so many of us actually have no sound criteria for judging between the Christian and the non-Christian, we have left ourselves wide open for the religious claims of the fanatic and of the fascist. It may seem strange to talk about fascism in the context of American democracy, and of course there are many safeguards, alongside the Christian religion, which have been built into the structure of our political society. Nevertheless, it should give us pause to realize that it was, *in part,* the uncritical religiosity of many pious German housewives which led them in the 1930's to accept Adolph Hitler as the new "Messiah" and to place his picture on their church altars. If American women are no more theologically discerning than were some of the German *Hausfrauen,* they lay themselves open to similar tragic possibilities. It is only as we know the actual theological content of our faith that we can discern between true religious claims and false ones, in whatever area of our life.

In the second place, because our theological understanding is often inadequate, we women have sometimes weakened the life of the very church we are trying to serve. It is we women who largely staff our voluntary Sunday school programs, guiding the worship and shaping the beliefs of every rising generation. Thus despite our burgeoning Christian education leadership programs— our teacher training and new curricula—it is usually we individual women Sunday school teachers who determine what religious tradition is passed on in the classroom on any given Sunday. Many women do a solid and sacrificial job, to be sure. Many thoroughly understand the Christian material they are teaching. But sadly enough, many, many more of us have failed to absorb even the basic fundamentals of Christian belief. We convey to the young only our own theological confusion. Sometimes this confusion is later dispelled in the child's home by theologically aware parents or on the student's college campus by a professor. But too often such confusion remains a permanent blight on the body of Christ.

Further, because we women in the church are often confused theologically, we frequently form one of the most immovable barriers to the growth and transformation of the church's life. The glib charge is often heard these days that the clergy are too conservative, that they have failed to keep pace with the demands of the twentieth century, and that they therefore cannot communicate to the common man or woman on the street. The truth is that the average seminary-trained clergyman is years ahead of most of his women members in his religious understanding. Not only is he, more often than not, thoroughly trained in traditional Christian theology, but he also has some understanding of the possible shapes which that theology can take in modern life. The clergyman, in his seminary study, has confronted and has evaluated 1,900 years of Christian practice. He usually knows where the church is now, why it got that way, and the direction in which it is moving. His battle consists sometimes in trying to persuade his women members to move along with it.

The clergyman's dilemma, however, is how on earth to appeal to those who do not understand the Christian faith, while yet remaining faithful to the Gospel to which he has been called to give his life—especially when those who lack understanding refuse to recognize their own lack or to take the necessary study steps to correct it. The clergyman cannot guide his congregation in terms of the vaguely thought-out goals so typical of some of his women members. He cannot propose a new program or worship life for the congregation on the grounds that it seems more "spiritual," that it will lead the members into "union with God," or that it will "do more good for more people." At least the clergyman cannot make such proposals and still keep his self-respect. By the nature of his calling, he must lead his congregation in terms of God's life among men. He must deal with the everyday realities of sin and forgiveness and restoration. He must justify his program and liturgy on the basis of God's act in Jesus Christ. He must look for motivation and guidance in terms of the working of the Holy Spirit among his members. Otherwise, the clergyman has simply sacrificed the gospel to ignorant expediency. The tragedy is that sometimes we women members, in our theological inadequacy, demand of him such a sacrifice. We fail completely to understand our minister's theological position and the goals which grow out of it. And thus, we criticize his leadership toward those goals and refuse to work in concert with him. Thinking ourselves active in the church, we women often condemn it to inaction. Judging ourselves self-righteously practical, we leave no room for the practice and action of God.

One of my critics has pointed out that there are often women in a congregation who have had courses in Bible and theology in college and who will come to the defense of their minister at such a time. But the tragedy is that our ministers must be attacked *at all* by those of us who are theologically inadequate and that the church must be disrupted *at any time* by the results of theological ignorance. Another critic has also accused me of being angry at women for our theological shortcomings. And I must confess that at times I do indeed become angry. I think our ministers deserve better than this. I think *all* our women are capable of more than this. And I certainly think the church of Jesus Christ must be served better than this.

Our theological inadequacies have had some other effects in our lives, however. If we go further in our examination of ourselves, it becomes clear that our weaknesses in understanding our faith have left many of us newly devoid of purpose. When we first began to take an active part in the mission and social outreach of the church, we had no doubt of our purpose. We were setting out on the great adventure of winning the whole world for Christ. We intended, by education and good works, to Christianize society at home. We intended, through foreign missions, to spread the gospel to every country on the face of the globe. Occasionally, national or international catastrophes interrupted our progress toward these goals. But it is significant that these catastrophes, such as the First World War and the 1929 stock market crash, were considered to be only interruptions. In February, 1935, the *News Bulletin* of the National Council of Federated Church Women contained the following quotation from the Spiritual Life Department:

With the improvement of economic conditions, let us not allow our people to lose track of things spiritual from their lives.

Have you allowed any financial depression to injure first of all your greatest enterprise, the evangelization of the world, while you kept yourselves safe and snug at home?

We church women, in the 1930's, were still largely confident that the kingdom lay just around the corner, and that we had embarked on the course which was leading the world to find it. Our determined march toward our goal filled us with a sense of joyful purpose and hope.

Then came the Hitler era and the horrors of Jewish annihilation, the spread of Marxist materialism and the clanging down of the Iron Curtain, the seething unrest of the growing giants of Asia and Africa, the militancy of a reawakened Islam dominating the Middle East, the renewal of Hinduism in a neutrally disdainful India, the revelation of a seemingly impenetrable poverty and instability in Central and South America. Suddenly we women—along with our men—became aware of a possibility of evil never known before in the world, a possibility symbolized by a cremation oven and a mushrooming atomic cloud. The kingdom of God appeared no longer an imminent reality. It seemed now remote and almost impossible of achievement. Furthermore, all those friendly lands known to us through our mission pamphlets were suddenly seen to be neither very friendly nor predominantly Christian. The gospel appeared to be a very small Word among many other conflicting words. The evangelization of the world seemed an overwhelming task, with no end to it in sight.

At home, moreover, we women found that American society had not so suddenly yielded to the persuasion of good works. The incidences of juvenile delinquency and of major crimes continued their alarming rise. Accustomed sex mores and family patterns suffered alarming breakdowns. Materialism failed to yield to the call to the spiritual. Our gentle admonitions to be loving and good went unheard in the rush to get ahead.

In short, we American church women had our Christian purpose and practice called into question by the events of recent history. The effect was to leave us troubled beyond our understanding. Had we been theologically grounded, we might have taken the logical course of questioning ourselves as to the validity of our religious presuppositions. We might have asked if it lies in our hands to establish the kingdom of God. We might have raised some fundamental questions about the ways of God in the world and the actual responsibilities laid upon us by the Lord of the church. But we simply did not have the theological insight to ask or to answer such questions. We therefore were plunged into troubled doubt, and some of us into a void of meaninglessness.

Our reactions to this crisis did little to solve our basic problem, however, and in many cases, they only accentuated it. Having been disillusioned with the results of spirituality and good works, many of us decided that we simply had not been spiritual and good enough. We judged that our efforts to save the world had failed not because they were misguided, but because they had not been carried out with enough faith and love. The call went out for better faith and greater zeal, and much of the resurgence of the church in the United States during the 1950's could be laid to this call "to try a little harder." It was a little like telling a sick person that his faith had failed to heal him only because his faith had not been quite strong enough to overcome his disease. All that seemed required was greater effort and greater belief. We women reassured ourselves time and again that in such religion lay the answer to the world's otherwise insoluble problems.

It is not surprising that such reasoning left many of us feeling nothing more than guilt—guilt because we could not believe quite strongly enough, guilt because in the rush of life we often neglected the "spiritual." It would be difficult to count all of the women's programs which in the past decade have laid before us American females the account of what we must do religiously in order to bring salvation to our troubled times. We have been told that we must have times of rest and times of meditation, "quiet hours" and regular retreats and "conversations with God," sacrificial stewardship disciplines including the willingness to participate in church activities, personalities radiant with the spiritual effects of "daily walks with God." Many of us have agreed that such religious exercises are, indeed, what we and our world need. But nevertheless, we women have failed to adopt such "necessities" in our daily lives. We therefore feel guilty because we believe that somehow we are failing our world. We are not doing the very things which so many have told us would bring salvation. Thus to our disillusionment and loss of purpose we have added a sense of personal and spiritual inadequacy. Such religion has become for many of us little more than a source of frustration.

We American women have reacted in other ways to the crisis generated by our loss of purpose. Most notably, we have adopted substitute goals toward which to direct our lives. One rarely hears in women's groups these days about building the kingdom of God. But there is a great deal of talk about building "a just and lasting peace." Now certainly the church is dedicated to the cause of peace in the world, and we should bend every effort to insure that a just peace becomes a reality for all peoples. But the significant fact is that these two goals—the kingdom and world peace—have become almost identical in the minds of many church women. Many among us are convinced that support of the American democratic way of life is at the same time support of the will of God. By their own peculiar manner of reasoning, such women have not really given up working to establish the kingdom on earth. But they have cloaked the kingdom in the outward trappings of national interests. They have made the kingdom of God visible on earth, as it were, and they now simply seek to extend its life, in the form of peaceful democracy, across the face of the earth. It remains, to be sure, a distant and difficult goal. Yet it is seemingly just a little more tangible, a little more obtainable, a little more relevant than that of winning the world for Christ. It is something that can be furthered by such concrete measures as those of supporting the United Nations or backing foreign aid. Almost any good cause can be viewed as contributing to it. Indeed, for the women to whom "peace" has become the sum total of the gospel, nothing is worth doing unless it contributes toward that fervently hoped-for goal. The acceptable ways of reaching the goal may depend on the woman's politics—some support the United Nations, for example, while others feel it an instrument of Satan. Nevertheless, world peace is for many women in America the new purpose and goal of their religion. World peace has become for many among us the synonymous substitute for the kingdom of Heaven.

Others have substituted for the goal of the kingdom another kind of peace, namely the goal of peace of mind and of contentment in their personal lives. Having been disillusioned in their attempts to evangelize the world, these women have turned inward in the search for rest for their troubled souls. Not a little of this turning has been due to the popularization of modern psychology. But even more it has been prompted by the lack of purpose many church women feel. Some among us frankly have no idea what they can do to help the world. They feel small and insignificant in the face of the era's complexities. They understand little of the church's life or role in the twentieth century. The only course left open to them is to seek religion's comfort.

We American women are assured reepatedly that religion can comfort us. Indeed, we are promised that religion can bring us wholeness and joy, transforming our personalities and making us into serene and imperturbable souls. Consider the following quotation from a recent religious book for women:

When perfectly attuned, a life is filled with harmony, even as music is brought forth from wood and catgut if the tension is exact. Perhaps

31

Christ—his spirit of love and light, of truth and beauty—is the violin bow waiting to bring the divine touch.[4]

It is indeed "harmony" that thousands of us in the church are seeking, that joyful, confident, serene existence we have been told is possible to us. Some among us seek such harmony through the medium of naturalism, as is typified so well in these words from the same author quoted above:

The peril of the modern woman is that she fails to take time to let her personality grow through solitude that gives pause for the development of the self through creating, imagining, loving, listening inwardly. Time to daydream, time to sit enfolded in peaceable greenness intent on the liquid song of a wood thrush, can germinate new life and make her whole.[5]

Or some among us seek harmony through the traditional medium of prayer, but prayer which has been transformed into a silent, mystical experience:

Prayer too often becomes a clamorous thing. We do all the talking. We do not listen enough. We fail to await the answer. Far too many times we do not expect it. If we would only "study to be quiet," to "be still, and know that [he is] God," even as he has told us thus to do, out of that silence would come his answer clear and plain. His voice would speak peace to our troubled hearts, and we would find the rest we so crave.[6]

The difficulty is that we women who search for peace of mind and rest and harmony often find that the objects of our search elude us. As one woman put it at the end of a ten-day sacrificial retreat

[4] Josephine Moffett Benton, *The Pace of a Hen* (Philadelphia: The Christian Education Press, 1961), p. 85.
[5] *Ibid.*, p. 86.
[6] Crowell, *Meditations*, p. 78.

of silence: "I found only myself." And the self we women are left with often remains troubled and unpeaceful. It might be shocking to us to hear that God would sometimes rather have us troubled than serene. But it might also jar us loose from the belief that our personal salvation is a valid substitue for the community of the kingdom. The "peace of mind" cult in America has given forth the unsavory fruit of self-centeredness and individualism. In the process it has done little to fill the void and lack of purpose present in the lives of so many of us.

2.

One of the most disturbing facts about the American woman's present religious situation is that our theological inadequacies have left us devoid of purpose at a time when, culturally, we desperately need religion's sustaining sense of meaning. No role in our society has undergone more changes in the past few decades than has the role of the female. And these changes have confronted the American woman with totally new problems. Indeed, they too have contributed to our loss of a sense of purpose.

On an educational and, to some extent, economic and political level, the United States' society has granted its women great freedom—the freedom to develop our abilities almost to the maximum extent possible. Especially has this been true in our schools and colleges, where women enjoy full freedom of opportunity and equal status with men. But on the social and marital level, women are not afforded the same freedom. We still are regarded as the subordinate partner to the dominant male. In most marriages in the United States it is taken for granted that the male's interests should be served, that his development of his talents should come before the development of those of his wife. The husband should be the one who "succeeds," while his wife lives through his achievement. The female's role should be largely that of encouraging and furthering her husband, of staying home to care for his house and to raise his children. For this reason, the United States' society as a whole deplores "the working wife," despite the now well-documented fact that the economy would collapse without her.[7] For the same reason, our society looks down on the spinster, the unfortunate soul whom it feels has failed to attain woman's proper place.

In fact, so "proper" does American society feel woman's place in the home to be, that from childhood on little girls are taught that they have one goal in life—the attainment of marital status, the securement of a home and family of their own. Their picture books and playthings all hold before them the ideal of home-maker. Their adolescent years are devoted to teaching them physically and socially how to get along with males. Rarely is there the suggestion that they should prepare themselves for any role outside of their homes, except perhaps in the "women's jobs" of nursing or teaching. Indeed, even the unmarried teacher or nurse is really considered to have missed her calling, namely her appropriate role as a wife and mother.

To be sure, our society is glad to educate its women, but their education can then have only three legitimate purposes in the eyes of that society. Women can use their education (1) to enrich their personal lives as wives and mothers; (2) to help put their husbands through college or graduate or technical school; (3) to support themselves in case they meet with failure, by which is meant, in case they fail to marry or to maintain their homes intact. In other words, women's education is not intended to fit them for their principal role in life. It is intended only to supplement that role or to come in handy as an emergency measure.

Whatever we may think of this attitude toward women in so-

[7] See the study on *Womanpower* by the National Manpower Council (New York: Columbia University Press, 1957).

ciety—and heaven deliver us from the professional feminists!—the fact is that it has left many of us women with an inner frustration and sadness almost beyond expression.[8] It is true that we American women still find our principal joys within the context of our homes. We would not trade our role as wives and mothers for any other or any thing. Nevertheless, wifehood and motherhood cannot fully satisfy the modern American woman, for as her educational opportunities have grown, she has learned the joy of "workmanship." She has experienced, on an equal educational level with men, the challenge of putting learning to use, of being engrossed and finding commitment to a task or a skill, of discovering and creating out of knowledge carefully assessed and gained. But once the American female enters the realm of marriage, she is largely expected to put this joy in workmanship behind her. The care of her house and husband, and devotion to her children—these are now expected to employ the whole of her talents and learning. The fact that they do not do so comes as a deep shock to most of us, and indeed, to most of our husbands. We women have been led to expect that husband and children will satisfy all of our needs. Instead, we find very often that homemaking consumes only a small part of our energies and interests and potentialities.

Modern labor-saving devices have certainly rid women of a great deal of drudgery. Precooked and prepared foods and factory-made clothes have made the necessities of life easily attainable. But the result has been to leave American women feeling very often unoccupied at home.[9] It really does not take much effort on our

[8] For an excellent discussion of the subject, see "Growing Up Female" by Bruno Bettelheim in a special supplement, on "The American Female," to *Harper's Magazine,* Oct., 1962, Copyright by Harper & Row, Inc. I am indebted to Dr. Bettelheim for many of my views stated above.

[9] Cf. a typical expression of this feeling on the part of housewife Mrs. Fred Biklé of Littleton, Colo., in the *Time* Letters-to-the-Editor column, Oct. 23, 1964, p. 14: "As a profession, housewifery may be noble as hell, but as a day to day occurrence, it is rather vapid."

parts to carry on the affairs of our households. To be sure, we still have the care and nurture of our children. But even the raising of the young cannot absorb the full attention of most educated women, and for the psychological sake of the young, it probably should not be expected to do so. As a result, we women often turn to community activities to occupy our time, though very often we find no real commitment or lasting purpose to such activities. Others among us, in increasing numbers, take part- or full-time jobs, despite the fact that our society as a whole disapproves of our working. Some of us adopt artistic and cultural pursuits. But no matter how we attempt to fill up our lives, the fact remains that large numbers of us continue frustrated and restless. In our education we have gained knowledge and abilities far exceeding our opportunities to use them. The effect is to leave many among us feeling as if they are merely "vegetating" at home. We want desperately to feel that we are needed and committed, not only as wives and mothers, but as fully trained, educated, responsible persons. We want deep down in our beings to be absorbed and engrossed in tasks which will call forth from us the full range of our talents. The fact is that few are presently so absorbed and engrossed. As a group, middle-class, educated American females lack an approved and yet purposeful role in our society. When this fact is combined with our loss of religious purpose, the result can portend trouble, not only in our personal lives, but in our homes, in our relations with our husbands and children, and in society at large.

It would be fallacious to maintain that a recovery of valid religious meaning and goals would solve all of the problems of American women. Clearly some of those problems will yield only to new views of woman's place in our changing society. But it is equally clear that a recovery of valid religious purpose could do a great deal to assist us through the period of transition and adjustment.

The Christian faith does not furnish all of the answers to life's problems, and it was never intended to do so. Indeed, it often raises more questions about our manner of living than it answers. But at the same time, biblical faith does supply a context to life from which changes and adjustments and difficulties can be viewed and dealt with. It is this context, this perspective, this theological ground of solidity that we American women sorely need today.

More than the American woman's *need* is at stake in grappling with our theological inadequacies, however. For we Christian women are not called by our Lord to concentrate on our own needs. It is not because we need our faith to get us through the day that we believe in Jesus Christ. Nor was it primarily to serve our needs that the Savior died on the cross. God is not the servant of man; man is the servant of God. And Jesus Christ humbled himself, taking the form of a servant, in order perfectly to serve not our needs, but the purpose of God.

To the same purpose, after the manner of the servitude of Christ, we Christian women are called. We are called to offer our lives as our Lord offered his. We are called to proclaim God's purpose, revealed in Jesus Christ. We are called to serve God's lordship, made certain in the person of his Son. But many of us cannot offer or proclaim or serve in our present religious state. Either we do not know what we believe or we are frustrated, and sometimes destroyed, by our errors. Blown by the winds of religiosity, disturbed by the whirlwinds of change, many of us have yet to find that Rock, who is much more a foundation upon which to stand than a shelter behind which to hide. Few of us are yet able to say with Paul, "I *know* whom I have believed." And because many of us do not know our Lord, in the theological, biblical sense of knowing, we are at the present time also unable adequately to follow him. Our theological inadequacies affect not only our relationships

37

with ourselves and our world. Our theological inadequacies affect first and foremost our relationships with our God.

It seems to me that now is the time to do something about our weaknesses in understanding our Christian faith. Women have a notable record of service to the church and to the Lord, to be sure. But we can seek "a still more excellent way." We can turn with renewed dedication to a study of our faith, in order that we may more adequately know whom it is we have believed.

This book is designed as a help along the way. Along with many, many other books, and pamphlets, and study materials, and curricula from our churches, it attempts to make more clear the content of the Christian proclamation. As only one guide among many to theological understanding, this book does not pretend to have an exclusive corner on the truth. But it is hoped that it will point the way toward greater theological insight, so that by the grace of God, we women may see more clearly "the light of the knowledge of the glory of God in the face of Christ."

CHAPTER II
SAINTS UNAWARE

Perhaps our basic difficulty in understanding the Christian faith has been our failure to understand adequately the nature of our relationship to God. Most women have a deep consciousness of the fact that they should be religious. Our difficulty is that we do not know exactly how to be religious. We need to know how to relate ourselves to our God. We need to know how God has related himself to us. Such knowledge would dispel a good deal of our theological confusion.

Many among us are convinced that God enters into relationship with them only in some so-called "mystical" or "spiritual" experience. They seriously believe that all true faith is based on a first-hand awareness of some sort of "presence" of God. They therefore expect to experience such "presence," and their religious activities are directed toward the cultivation of such an experience. The communal worship of such groups of women is seen largely as an emotional affair. An inspiring speaker or moving music or a touching liturgy is employed, in order to induce in the worshipers an emotional experience of God's nearness. Most important, however, is the individual's inner relationship to God. These women acclaim, and at the same time almost envy, anyone with a mystical talent. Their heroes are those who can exercise what Brother Lawrence has called "the practice of the presence of God." Their leaders are women who can penetrate this physical world into the "beyond." The woman who has heard the voice of God in prayer, the one who reports an overwhelming manifestation of God's physical presence in her life, even the hostess who always puts the empty chair at her table for the "Unseen Guest"—these are the ones who are considered religious by this mystical, experiential brand of faith. The females who follow them listen almost wistfully as they "witness" to their spiritual experiences. For most women have had, they will confess, very few such experiences of their own.

Other women have a different view of religion. They believe that they can enter into relationship with God only by complete surrender. Faith for them is based upon a unique moment of dedication, when all they have and are is turned over to Jesus Christ. The religious heroes of these women are not the mystics or spiritualists. Their heroes are largely drawn from the missionary ranks of the church. Thus, for example, they see in Albert Schweitzer a supreme example of dedication, in that Schweitzer left behind him fame and comfort to live in the jungles of Africa. In other instances they idolize Tom Dooley, or Kagawa of Japan, and they feel that the dedication of such men is the true way of religion. Faith involves the sacrifice of one's own comfort and security, the giving up of all one has in the service of the Master.

Women who see their relationship to God to be based upon

such dedication, often hold within them the conviction, therefore, that "someday they will be truly Christian." They frequently secretly harbor the thought of a moment in the distant future when they will make one final glorious surrender to Christ and become ever after his servants. Some day, they tell themselves, they will give themselves up completely, joining the ranks of those heroes who have given their all for the Lord. In the meantime, they satisfy themselves with partial dedications and surrenders. But they really do not feel that these relate them totally to their God.

Another segment of womanhood strives for relationship to God by asceticism, by the practice of extraordinary devotional and stewardship rites. Their key thought is "sacrifice," the sacrifice of persons and time and money. They are sticklers for "duty" and "discipline" and "participation" in religious activities. Only if religion interrupts all the normal procedures of life has it become sufficiently central in the thought of these women. The relationship to God, for them, can be established only at a cost. They are zealous that they and their associates daily pay the price.

I encountered an example of this view of faith as a student on the Stanford campus. Muriel Lester, the noted English religious leader, gave a talk to a group assembled to profit from her example. In this talk she explained the nature of true devotion. "The real test of your faith," she said, "is how early you are willing to get up to pray." She suggested that perhaps five A.M. would be a reasonable rising hour each morning. I recall that as a student, I was much impressed by her statement. Now as a mother of two young children, I can only conclude that if this be faith's only possibility, I and millions of housewives like me are among the lost.

This is not to deprecate the real religious contribution of people like Muriel Lester. It certainly is not intended to castigate or caricature the religious practices of thousands of women. There is a large place in the Christian faith for the experience of the presence of God, for dedicated surrender to Christ, and for zealous duty and discipline. But the theological error of many women is that they believe their experience, or surrender, or sacrifice is the *basis* for their relationship to God. And those who propagate such beliefs lead countless fellow females astray. There is no crueler hoax that can be perpetrated upon a suffering or troubled woman than to tell her that she can find her God only by having a "spiritual experience." She usually has no strength left in her to try to find anyone, and the effect is to consign her to even greater helplessness and guilt. It is time that we women learn enough theology to avoid such cruelty.

The fact is that our relationship to God is not dependent on our religious experiences or on the quality of our dedication or on the extent of our sacrifice. It is not dependent on anything we believe or feel or do. Our relationship to God is dependent on Jesus Christ. And without God's act in Jesus Christ, there can be no relationship.

It is not only ignorant to believe that we can enter into fellowship with the living God by using some technique of worship or practice. It is irreligious and blasphemous to believe so. For this God whom we worship is not so slavishly at our beck and call. We can experience his presence in our lives only if he wills to be present. We can enter into relationship with him only if he desires to be known by us.

A friend has often reminded me that the concepts of monarchies or kingships are alien to American thought in our age. And yet there are few terms which describe the God of the Bible any better in his revelation of himself than does the title "King." The God of the biblical, Judaic-Christian faith is the King or Lord of the universe. In the words of the prayer of Jesus, his is "the kingdom and the power and the glory." He is described by the prophet Isaiah as "high and lifted up" (Isa. 6:1), so glorious in his majesty that the seraphim must veil their faces in his presence (Isa. 6:2), so righteous in his holiness that the prophet feels immediately sinful before him (Isa. 6:5). His power is such that he reigns over all the nations (Ps. 47:8), bringing princes to nought and making the rulers of the earth as nothing (Isa. 40:23). At the command of his voice, the very earth can melt (Ps. 46:6). All nature is but a tool to praise his justice and truth (Pss. 96:11-13; 98:7-9). When a vision of his glory and power is granted to Ezekiel, the prophet can only fall prostrate to the ground, unable to speak or hear until commanded by the Lord to rise (Ezek. 1:28-2:2).

Moreover, God's kingly goodness brings such salvation to the world that even the messenger announcing his coronation must be celebrated by a hymn:

How beautiful upon the mountains
are the feet of him who brings good tidings,
who publishes peace, who brings good tidings of good,
who publishes salvation,
who says to Zion, "Your God reigns" (Isa. 52:7).

It is little wonder that the birth of God's Son is pictured as heralded by the songs of the heavenly host (Luke 2:10-14), and that the lowliest procession of Jesus and his followers is interpreted as a royal triumph parade (Matt. 21:1-11). This God and Father of our Lord Jesus Christ is "King of kings and Lord of lords." A Hallelujah Chorus of praise and honor is the proper response to his royal presence.

Because the God of biblical faith is indeed our King, our Lord, our Ruler, we do him no service by thinking we can enter lightly into his presence. You do not honor a king by demanding your right to an audience. And we do not honor God by trying to shove our way into his presence.

Throughout its pages the Bible is aware of our intimate relationship to God, to be sure. From the very first, the people of faith are considered not only servants, but also sons of God (cf. Exod. 4:22-23). God bears for them the love of a Father (Jer. 31:20; Hos. 11:1). God is as closely related to his people as is a husband to his wife (Isa. 54:4-5). And yet biblical faith never is guilty of our dissipation of the love of God. Because God loves us with the affection of a father or husband does not mean that he is any less our King or Lord. Rather, it is precisely because God is Lord that his husbandly tenderness is all the more astounding (Isa. 54:1-8). It is precisely because God is King and Master that his fatherhood is to be praised and honored (Mal. 1:6). What does it matter that God is our Father if he has no power and authority? Of what importance is the news that he loves us if he is impotent to rule us in love? Love which has no power to become effective remains a weak and frustrated emotion. The Bible starts first with the proclamation of the kingly power and authority of God.[1] Its good news, then, is that the King of the universe is at the same time a King of love.

We women need to examine ourselves in relation to God the King. For it is very clear that we have considered ourselves worthy to go rushing into his courts. Seeking an emotional thrill or strength for the day, we have presumptuously summoned the King to be with us. Desiring to prove ourselves dedicated Christians, we have

[1] Some scholars would disagree with this statement, maintaining that the Bible begins with a proclamation of God's love and redemption, e.g. in the exodus from Egypt. However, there is no act of redemption in the Bible which is not at the same time understood as a manifestation of God's kingly power to rule. The exodus serves as a revelation of God's lordship over the forces of both nature and men, as well as a revelation of God's love for Israel. Even the covenant ceremony and stipulations, by which God enters into relationship with Israel at Sinai, have been shown to be modeled after ancient Hittite treaties, in which a king entered into relationship with his vassals. From the very first, God was considered to be King over Israel, and it is his authority and power as King which we have forgotten in our proclamation of his love. (For evidence of God's early kingship, cf. the ancient conception of the ark as the throne of the invisible God, Num. 10:35-36; I Sam. 4:4.)

written the King's laws for living for him. Deciding before hand what will please the King, we have proclaimed his will far and wide, seldom bothering to distinguish carefully between *his* will and *our* will. It is no accident that we consider the biblical admonition to "fear the Lord" an outdated and erroneous approach to God. For biblical "fear" is awe and respect before the power and authority of the King of kings. We consider that King a serf to be summoned or a puppet for the execution of our desires. We have little idea what the psalmist means when he summons us to worship with these words: "The Lord reigns; let the peoples tremble!" (Ps. 99:1.) "Why should we tremble?" is our response, "After all, he's only a God of love!"

By this very attitude we women declare ourselves sinners before God. The ease with which we think to enter God's presence makes us unworthy to do so. For sin in the Bible is not primarily a specific immoral act. It is not first of all the violation of some ethical code. It is not principally the failure to do some good or to avoid some wrong. Rather, sin in the Bible is above all rebellion, the refusal or the failure to acknowledge the kingship of God. Sin is the attempt to make God less than he is, namely, less than the absolute Lord over all of life. It is saying, "Thine is not the kingdom and the power and the glory." It is acting as if his kingdom will not come and as if his will will not be done. It is the refusal to hallow his name, that is, the refusal to acknowledge his absolute lordship in every thought and word and deed.

To use another example, we women very often make clear our sin in our awful deeds of pride. We are so pharisaically sure that we know what is right and wrong. We engrave our tinny tablets with our rigid little ethical codes, and then we slander and gossip and cluck our tongues over those who fail to conform. How shocked we would have been by that nonconformist named Jesus! How we would have kept our telephones ringing to report his visits to prostitutes! How we would have organized a committee to investigate his conversations with un-American publicans! And we would have done it all, like the Pharisees and scribes and Sadduccees, in the name of our religion.

There is more truth than fiction in that ancient story of Woman in the Garden of Eden. For her temptation was to "be like God, knowing good and evil" (Gen. 3:5). She was not content to abide by the commands that the Lord of her life had given her. In her reply to the serpent (Gen. 3:3), she added a little law of her own.[2] She infringed just a bit on God's prerogative to rule over her life. Finally, she cast aside his command altogether (Gen. 3:6) and attempted to control her own destiny. She wanted to be her own master, making God unnecessary. Her sin was her attempt to usurp God's rule and to replace it with her own.

Every time we modern women set up our own codes of respectability and right, we bear the sin and name of Eve. For it is clear that God the King is not limited by our middle-class morality. His compassion reaches out beyond the boundaries of etiquette and dress and propriety, to accept the poor, the awkward, the unacceptable, and the practitioners of the *faux pas*. The concern of God is heedless of Emily Post propriety, and every time we identify polite with right we risk rebellion against his rule. Our snobbishness, our pride, our judgment and ostracism of our fellows, brand us females with the label of "subversive" in the kingdom of God.

To be sure, such pride is only one example of our rebellion against our Lord. But it makes quite clear the overall character of what the Bible means by sin. Sin against God is our attempt to write our own rules, to have the last word as to how our society and marriages and homes and children and lives in general should be run. Sin is substituting our will for the will of God, no matter

---

[2] Specifically, in her assertion that God has forbidden her to touch the tree, Eve goes beyond the original commandment given her by the Lord (cf. Gen. 2:17).

what the issue or decision involved. It is making our opinions
(even our opinions about ourselves!), our principles, our judgments
the absolute measures of good. It is denying that God's is the final
power and authority. It is failing to believe and act as if God is the
King over life.

If we women would be Christians, we must be aware of the rule
of God, both in the daily practice of our faith and in the formula-
tion of our beliefs. We deny the kingship of God not only by
what we do. We deny his kingship also by what we believe. It is
blasphemous to think we can summon God to be present whenever
we wish him near, just as it is blasphemous to try to replace his
authority with our own. God cannot be summoned or replaced by
anyone, much less by us—rebels in his realm. And only if God himself desires to come to us can we enter into relationship with him.
We are dependent completely on his lordly will, because he, not man,
is the King and Ruler of all of life.

There is not much meaning, therefore, to the effort to make
ourselves religious. No woman is "spiritual" or "dedicated" or
"Christian" unless God has chosen to enter into relationship with
her. And then the relationship has been established by God and
not by her efforts and desires. No religious leader deserves any
envy or acclaim. If she is truly religious, she is but a sign of the
action of God. If she has built her own reputation, she is a denial
of his lordship, a modern example of the biblical story of the Tower
of Babel. "Come," ran the call of mankind at the place of Babel
(Gen. 11:1-9), "let us build ourselves a city, and a tower with its
top in the heavens, and let us make a name for ourselves" (Gen.
11:4). The "religious" woman, who thinks to earn or to prove her
relationship to God, is once again trying to erect that tower of pride,
with its top in the heavens. She is trying to make a name for herself, when it is God's act alone that deserves our praise. God the

King seeks out and finds whom he will (cf. Exod. 33:18-23). We are dependent on his initiative for our fellowship with him.

This is not to say that we must not respond to God's initiative. And it is not to say that some women do not respond in faith and dedication and devotion to God's prior act, while other women seem to turn away from God altogether. We have mentioned earlier that the responses of devotion and discipline and duty have a large place in the Christian faith. We will later discuss our responsibilities for response. But let us be clear at the outset that *we* do not set up our relationship with God. It is the divine King alone who can initiate our relationship with him.

Biblical faith, then, starts with the proclamation of the kingship of God. That proclamation brings a judgment upon our views of religion. It castigates our easy spirituality, our rebellious prides, and our sinful claims to superior devotion. It puts us in our proper place as rebels undeserving of entrance into the courts and kingdom of God. It illumines for us our sin over against God the King. It leaves us without a ghost of a chance of relationship with our Lord.

1.

The amazing fact of biblical faith is that despite our sin and rebellion, despite our unworthiness to enter into the presence of our Lord, God declares us acceptable to him and welcomes us into his fellowship. Indeed, the Bible goes far beyond our own self-views and the world's estimation of us. The Bible has the audacity to call you and me by the name of "saint"!

Now I don't know about you, but by the common definition of sainthood, the title "saint" is certainly a misnomer for me! John Henry Cardinal Newman has defined it in the following manner:

Why were the saints, saints? Because they were cheerful when it was difficult to be cheerful, patient when it was difficult to be patient;

and because they pushed on when they wanted to stand still, and kept silent when they wanted to talk, and they were agreeable when they wanted to be disagreeable. That was all. It was quite simple, and always will be.

Such a manner of living may have seemed simple to John Henry Newman. When a woman is tired from nursing a sick child all night, or has had a fight with her husband, being cheerful and patient, and silent and agreeable does not seem at all so simple. Clearly, such a definition is not what the Bible has in mind. In fact, it applies the name of saint to the most ungodly persons.

Consider for example Paul's first letter to the Corinthians. In his opening sentences, Paul writes to the "saints" in Corinth, but the rest of his letter portrays a congregation far from our usual picture of sainthood. He accuses the Corinthian Christians of quarreling and jealousy and strife, of inner divisions within their church, caused by proud boasts of superiority (I Cor. 1:10-12; 3:3-4, 18-23). He reveals that some are guilty of sexual irregularities (5:1) and traffic with prostitutes (6:15-16). He mentions that others are taking their fellow Christians into court (6:1). Some have even been stuffing themselves or getting drunk at the Lord's Supper (11:21). This is the roistering, quarrelsome, immoral lot, which Paul entitles "saints." The term quite obviously has a different meaning in the Bible than that to which we are accustomed. It has nothing to do with our usual definition of moral perfection or superiority.

In the original language of the Scriptures three words are used for "saint": *hasid* and *qâdôsh* in the Hebrew Old Testament, and *hagios* in the Greek New Testament. All of these words have a common basic meaning. They signify one that is "holy," by which is meant, one that is set apart for God's use. That is, a saint is a person who is taken into God's realm and reserved there for God's special purpose. A saint is a person who is accepted by God and marked out for a special function. This is what the Bible means when it calls you and me by the title "saints." We are, first of all, acceptable to God. We are allowed to enter into his holy realm. We have the opportunity to enter the presence of the King of kings.

Despite our sin and unworthiness, despite our rebellion against the Lord, he bestows on us the name of "saints" and welcomes us into his kingdom. And the reason for this paradoxical action by God is found in Jesus Christ. Because of Christ, you and I are now acceptable to God.

There are many different theological explanations of the saving work of Jesus Christ, and all of them have some justification in the biblical text. Some say that Christ died in our place, receiving the punishment due all our sins, and thus we now are considered guiltless and pure before God. Others talk in terms of ransom paid to personified Evil: Christ as the only righteous and innocent person did not deserve to die, but yet offered himself to the powers of evil to buy our release from them. Still others interpret the cross of Christ from the standpoint of the Old Testament understanding of an atoning sacrifice: the lifeblood of Jesus is the efficacious gift which God himself gives on our behalf to make us pleasing to him. Or others speak in biblical terms of a covenant: the body and blood of Christ, as symbolized in the Lord's Supper, are the elements binding us together with God and each other in an unbreakable covenant of life. Finally, some interpreters of the history of Jesus Christ talk in terms of a cosmic event: in his life and crucifixion, the Son of God meets the universal powers of evil head on, winning God's victory over them in the resurrection from the dead. Through faith in the Son of God, therefore, we participate in his victory, and become free to enter into the presence and eternal life of God, bereft of our slavery to evil and to its accompanying death.

Some of these theological explanations are difficult for us to understand, especially since I have not stated them in their many details. Certainly no one explanation is sufficient in itself to interpret fully the nature of God's act in Jesus Christ. That act is of such ultimate importance and has such universal significance for all of us that it must be reinterpreted and newly explained for every generation and nation. But we can be clear about the most basic meanings of the event in Jesus Christ. We can firmly grasp the most central affirmations of the Christian faith.

In his Son Jesus Christ, God the King has forgiven us our rebellion against him. He has not said that we are without sin or that our rebellion makes no difference to him. He has not tried to make our rebellion less serious by masquerading as someone less than the Lord. God is really the King and Lord, and our sin has been the actual denial of his lordship. But nevertheless, in Jesus Christ, God has forgiven our sin. In his willingness to send his Son to die for us, in the outstretched sign of the cross, God has opened his arms and said to us simply, "Come! Come, no matter who you are or what you have done to me. Come, no matter how you feel or what you have believed. You are acceptable to me, through my Son. Through him, I will welcome and receive you."

We should carefully note, however, that God's act of forgiveness in Jesus Christ is not merely a proclamation which has been spoken. God has not sent his Son only to *tell* us of his love. Jesus is not just a messenger carrying the word of reconciliation. Jesus Christ is that Word. He is the forgiveness of God made flesh. He is the act of forgiveness taken place. With his death on the cross, his broken body has become the bridge of mercy, joining heaven and earth, and no matter what we may think of him, he has forever opened the way between sinful man and his God. The act has taken place. The deed of reconciliation has been wrought. By sending his Son into the world, God has effected our forgiveness.

In other words, the God of the Bible has refused to leave us alone.

51

Having seen our sinful rebellion and the chaos we have wrought in his realm, he has refused to remain aloof in his courts in unconcern or anger. Instead, he has sent his Son to seek us out and to give us the possibility of return. In the person of Christ God has come down off his throne and out into our life to find us.

Thus in everything done by Jesus of Nazareth, we see the forgiveness of God, and not only Christ's death, but also his life shows forth God's mercy in action. Consider the way Jesus constantly accepts the most unacceptable people. We find him eating with the drunkards and making friends with the prostitutes and leftists. We hear of him breaking the religious laws with the nonreligious and the social laws with the socially outcast. We discover that he takes the side of the poor and of the deformed, and that his special friends are the widow and the spinster. We read that even on the cross, he uses his last breaths of life to accept a thief and to forgive his executioners. But his acts are not simply those of an incredibly merciful, or perhaps naïve, man. They are the acts of God toward us in his amazing, forgiving love. In parable after parable, Jesus tells us that what he does is also that which God is doing toward us—accepting us despite our total unacceptableness. As Jesus acted on earth to accept the most rejected, so God the King acts toward us to search out and to welcome us sinners. Through Jesus Christ we rebels are found and forgiven by our Lord.

We have the invitation, then, to enter into the courts of God. In Jesus Christ we have God's act by which the doors into his presence are open. We lack only the strength and healing to rise up and follow Christ home. The Son has come to take us to his Father, but now we need new power to walk. Our old rebellions, our prides, our selfishness, our distaste for a ruler over us, still serve to glue us to the spot of our present disobedience. We are like cripples, with broken legs, invited to come to the royal feast.

Or we are like that paralytic, in the Gospel according to Mark, who heard that his sins were forgiven, and yet who lay, still immobilized, on his customary cot (Mark 2:1-12).

But the proclamation of Jesus to the paralytic was a declaration of power: "That you may know that the Son of man has authority on earth to forgive sins, . . . I say to you, rise, take up your pallet and go home" (Mark 2:10-11). The Gospel records that immediately the paralytic arose "and went out before them all" (Mark 2:12). It is with the same power that Jesus Christ forgives and seeks out us. He comes into our lives not with the frustrating announcement of a forgiveness we are powerless to utilize, not with the impotent appeal for us to "try a little harder," not with a useless invitation from the King which we are unable to answer, but with the authority and might to heal and to release us. The Lord of life is the King of power, and in the resurrection of Jesus Christ, he holds out to us the promise of victory over our infirmities. God, in his Son's resurrection, is stronger than death, stronger than evil, stronger than the paralysis of rebellion and pride and self-centeredness which would leave us helpless before the forces of destruction. And this strength he proffers to us in the person of his Son. God comes to us in Jesus Christ, accepting us and welcoming us, and at the same time providing us the power to take advantage of his invitation.

Let us not deceive ourselves and others, however. In Jesus Christ we women are not suddenly transformed into different and perfect creatures. Such a belief can lead us into terrible self-righteousness before the eyes of our fellows. Worst of all, it can lead us finally into despair about our continuing shortcomings. We remain, as Christians, still selfish and egotistical and full of desires to escape God's rule. We remain, until the kingdom comes, still subject to sin and imperfect. The women who claim to be otherwise are probably the fartherest from the kingdom of God. But in reliance

53

on Christ we no longer are bound and enslaved by the dark forces of our evil. We know that Christ has won the victory over them. Therefore, we do not indulge in destructive despair over our continuing inability to do the right. We are not laden with an anxious guilt which leads us to foolish and frantic self-justifications. We do not fear that some misstep of sin or unwitting weakness may lead us to destroy ourselves. Instead, we live day by day in the joyful knowledge that even our own evil ways cannot separate us from the love of God in Jesus Christ. We cannot be held captive by the shackles of sin or dragged into the dark of final destruction, because God in the resurrection of his Son has claimed us forever as his own. And he promises that no matter how dreadful the battle, we will be given his life and light. It is in this faith that we can live day by day, in wholeness and freedom and certainty. Because of Christ, we have the confidence and strength to go on. By the victory of Christ, we are given the power to continue the battle.

It is in this way, then, that you and I are saints. As Paul puts it in his letter to the Philippians, we are saints only by virtue of being "in Christ Jesus" (Phil. 1:1). We are acceptable to God the King only because of his Son. Without Jesus Christ we remain exactly what we humanly are—rebels who are unforgiven and displeasing to the King who has created us to serve him. But in his Son, our Lord has transformed our entire status before him. He has searched us out, forgiven our rebellion, and allowed us to come into his presence. We, the unacceptable, have been made acceptable to our Lord. We, the unsaintly sinners against him, have been granted the status of his saints.

It seems clear that if we accept this biblical proclamation of such good news by repentance and by trust in Christ, it can become a proclamation of freedom for us—freedom from the awful burden of piety and religiosity which so many wish to impose upon us. Our society has constructed a stereotype of whom it considers to be the religious person. In countless ways, in church and out, it seeks to impose that stereotype upon us. The religious person, it says, does this or doesn't do that. The religious person behaves and feels in one particular manner. The religious person is a "type," easily recognizable at a glance. And those who conform to the stereotype are rewarded with the labels of "spiritual" or "dedicated" or "Christian personality." The rest of us are left with the feeling that we remain outside the realm of the holy, strangers to the presence and real knowledge of our God.

To such thoughts and enslaving stereotype the good news of the Bible thunders "No! You are welcome," it proclaims to us, "into God's holy realm. By reason of God's act in Jesus Christ, you are now God's actual saints, received and welcomed by the love of God in Christ Jesus, into fellowship with your Lord."

If we cling to Jesus Christ, you and I are free, free from every pious judgment and religious law that someone else would impose upon us, free to revel in the glorious knowledge that we, too, have access to the throne of God, free to enter, just as we are, into the presence of our Lord. Let no woman claim to have superiority or precedence before her fellows when approaching the God of the Bible. None is acceptable to God except through Jesus Christ, and because of him, all are equally received. All of us women, no matter what our status or pattern of piety, can stretch our unfettered souls in "the glorious liberty of the children of God" (Rom. 8:21) and declare with the apostle Paul, "By the grace of God I am what I am" (1 Cor. 15:10). Such is the liberating fact of our sainthood in Jesus Christ.

2.

We must not forget, however, that our title of saint has a further meaning. It denotes not only the fact that we are acceptable to

God through Jesus Christ. It also means that we have been accepted by God to perform a specific function. It means that God has welcomed us into his fellowship for a particular purpose.

Many Christian women go astray in their understanding of the biblical faith because they fail to perceive the *purpose* of God's act in Jesus Christ. They feel that the life, death, and resurrection of God's Son are completely isolated events in human history. Jesus enters into the world, having no relationship to the events that have taken place before him. He lives on earth a little while, during which time he brings forgiveness and healing to all men. But then he returns to the life of heaven, and history continues apace, as a whole unaffected by the incarnation of the divine in human flesh.

In the context of such a view of Christ Christian faith is necessarily understood as individual and private. Its purpose is to appropriate in the life of each separate person those forgiving and healing benefits made available to individuals in the thirty isolated years that Jesus lived on earth. According to this view, each worshiper receives such gifts when he enters into a private relationship with God through Christ. In the recesses of his own soul, the individual receives inner healing. He then is expected to act outwardly better, thus bringing to bear upon the secular course of the world a moral and saving influence. Salvation will come on earth, it is held, when enough individuals are made Christian. And those who practice their faith on earth will at the last be received, as individual believers, into the eternal life of heaven.

In their total effect such beliefs present a compartmentalized, boxed-in understanding of God's work in the world. The Lord acts in a Savior from the blue, in an isolated span of time, to save the souls of particular individuals, privately and apart from normal life. Faith is a matter of a "little postern gate" within ourselves through which we enter into a realm apart from the world. God's work in Jesus Christ to save us all is an action unrelated to the rest of life.

In reality such views are a distortion of biblical faith, which puts the event of Jesus Christ firmly in the middle of flesh-and-blood history and which attaches to his incarnation far more than significance merely for individuals. Jesus Christ is, in the understanding of the Scriptures, the one through whom God fulfills his purpose for human life. And that purpose is to establish a new community which acknowledges the rule of God as Lord.

In a sense the whole story of the Bible is the story of man's destruction of community and God's restoration of it, for the Bible clearly recognizes that sin is more than an individual matter and that its cure must affect more than single souls. When Eve, who symbolizes all women, rebels against her God in Eden, her sin disrupts every normal relationship of her life. She has been created for joyful unity with her husband, as the one who is to complete his being and bear him children in love (Gen. 2:18, 23-25). But Eve's rebellion turns her relationship with Adam into one of shame (Gen. 3:7). Her role as childbearer becomes a source of pain and of possible death. Her very sexuality brings with it a humiliating domination by her mate (Gen. 3:16).

Likewise with Adam, the created goodness of his life is turned to evil by his sin. His work was originally given him to provide him with food and to satisfy his desire for creativity and beauty (Gen. 2:9, 15). When he rebels against God, his work becomes instead a source of drudgery, frustration, and tedium. The futility of it all is finally made clear in the *finis* that death writes to his struggle (Gen. 3:17-19). In the view of the Bible a radical disruption has entered life with man's rebellion against God, a disruption of the most basic relationships and processes of life.

This disruption is not limited to the circle of marriage. Its effects spread far beyond the original symbolic couple. In the story of Cain and Abel (Gen. 4:1-16) we find it infecting the relationship of brother to brother, with Cain rebelliously willing to murder in jealous irresponsibility toward God and man. In the short notice about Lamech (Gen. 4:19, 23-24) irresponsible rebellion becomes vengeful self-rule, with the power of God over life and death fully usurped by sinful man. In the story of the flood Eve's original naïve desire "to be like God, knowing good and evil," is found to have led to a state in which man knows only how to do evil (Gen. 6:5). And the universal consequences of man's infectious cancer of wrong finally are portrayed in the myth of the Tower of Babel (Gen. 11:1-9). Man's attempts to play God lead him into total chaos and disunity. Even communication between nation and nation becomes impossible. The picture is one in which man's relationships with his fellows and his world are, at every level, destroyed. Man's denial of the lordship of God means the breakdown of every form of community. The rebellion of sin brings with it radical and universal chaos.

The important fact, however, is that the Bible is saying that this is the nature of *our* world, for it deliberately applies the stories of Genesis 3-11 to you and to me. "Adam," in the Hebrew Old Testament, is the word for "mankind." The story of Adam's sin and its effects is meant to portray us. We live, the Bible is saying, in disrupted and broken community, and our chaos is due to our sinful flight from God's rule over us. Only when God's lordship is affirmed can there be a new community. And only in the restoration of community will the disease of man's sin be healed. There is no such thing as being "saved" by ourselves in the Bible. Sin's effect is to tear us asunder from our fellows and our world, and a purely individualistic view of religion simply deepens sin's infection. In the view of the Bible salvation is synonymous with the restoration of community, with the renewal of man's relationships with his world and fellows, under the lordship of God.

The proclamation of the Bible, then, from Genesis 12 onwards, concerns the actions of God, as he works in the life of man, toward his goal of creating for himself a new and faithful community. We are often shocked by the biblical view that God chose Israel (Exod. 19:4-6; Deut. 7:6-8; Rom. 9:4-5; 11:1-5). And yet this fact is simply a statement of the necessity and love of God: to make a new community on earth, he had to start somewhere with someone! He chose the orphan Israel (cf. Ezek. 16) because it would be very plain that her creation was due to God's efforts and not to her own (cf. Deut. 7:7). Other nations had their own might, their own laws, their own religions. God wanted to make a people that would be all his own.

Certainly Israel was insignificant before God got hold of her—a conglomerate scattering of adventurers and traders and semi-nomads, some of whom had fallen into slavery (Exod. 1). But it was in such weakness that the Lord of history could show forth his ruling might, and he set about to change this "no-people" of Israel into his new people of faith. He delivered them from those that enslaved them [3] and taught them the way to live together.[4] He battled before them in order to give them a new Eden "flowing with milk and honey" [5] (cf. Deut. 8:7-10). He set up a monarchy to govern them and to guarantee their security.[6] He sent them prophets to intercede for them and to keep them constantly in the way of the Word.[7]

The expectation of God as he poured out such care on Israel was that she would respond to him in gratitude and obedience and trust (cf. Isa. 5:1-7). Surely she would learn from his acts that she

[3] The story of the exodus (Exod. 1–15).

[4] The giving of the law through Moses on Mt. Sinai and in the desert of Moab (Exod. 20–Deut. 31).

[5] The story of the conquest of Canaan, under the leadership of Joshua (the book of Joshua).

[6] The story of David and his successors (I Sam. 16–II Chr. 35), after the period of the Judges (Judg. and I Sam. 1–12), and the rejection of the first king, Saul (1 Sam. 13–15).

[7] The prophetic books.

could rely on him for all things, including the way to conduct herself as a community in a hostile world (cf. Isa. 7:1-9). Surely she would recognize that he was in charge of life and that she had but to trust his kingly rule and power (cf. Isa. 30:1-17). And God planned, then, that Israel's faith would serve as a witness to all the world, as a witness to his power to create and to protect and to redeem. Indeed, God promised that if from the midst of suffering or destruction or exile, Israel would nevertheless proclaim his power to preserve and rescue her, all nations would be brought to the worship of her God (Isa. 40-55). This was the goal toward which God worked: the reconciliation of the world to himself through the instrument of his people Israel (cf. Isa. 2:2-4; 45), in short, the inclusion of all men and nations in his new community of faith (cf. Isa. 56:5-8; Zeph. 3:9; Zech. 8:20-23). God asked Israel to trust his lordship, even in the worst of circumstances, in order that all peoples might be led by her witness into the community of trust (Isa. 52:13-53:12).

The Old Testament itself repeatedly tells us, however, that Israel never could live up to the role of Suffering Servant assigned her by God. She simply did not trust her Lord (cf. Ps. 78). As the great empires of the ancient Middle East marched their armies toward her borders, she did "not look to the Holy One of Israel or consult the Lord" (Isa. 31:1). Instead, she went fluttering like a defenseless dove,

> silly and without sense,
> calling to Egypt, going to Assyria

for alliance and protection (Hos. 7:11; cf. 12:1). As the fields were sown and the rains were needed, Israel became anxious about God's ability to govern the forces of nature, and turned instead to the idols of the baals and astartes in the fertility cults of the Canaanites (Hos.

2:2-13). As tragedy came, and Jerusalem was destroyed, and war's survivors went into exile, Israel refused to believe that God's judgment and love were shaping the course of her life. Instead, she complained that God was unjust (Ezek. 18:29) and sank into hopelessness. "My way is hid from the Lord," she moaned, "and my right is disregarded by my God" (Isa. 40:27). At every turn, the people of God, created to witness to his lordship, refused to trust the power and willingness of their Lord to govern the events of their lives. God, they said, could not act, or he would not act. Israel's failure was a failure of faith in the loving rule of God the Lord—the rebellious attempt to replace his acts with her own expedient efforts toward salvation. In her disbelieving attempt to save herself, Israel lost her life. "For whoever would save his life will lose it, and whoever loses his life for my sake will find it" (Matt. 16:25). Because Israel refused to live in trust of God's lordship, he gave her over to judgment and to death (cf. e.g. Isa. 6:9-13; Jer. 1:13-16; Ezek. 9; Amos 9:1-4, *etc.*).

God's destruction of Israel, however, did not mean the end of his working. Nor did it signify the abandonment of his goal of a new community of faith. The Lord of history cannot be defeated by man's rebellious unbelief. And he has no intention of leaving us as we are in our chaotic and broken world. God is always acting in the sphere of our life, always shaping history to overcome our sinful rebellion, always pressing forward in love to make a new people under his lordship. And the very prophets who announced Israel's destruction also proclaimed these facts. Straining their vision beyond the shackles and ruins of an old Israel, dying in exile, the prophets perceived the outlines of a new Israel become faithful to its ruling Lord (Zeph. 3). God, they said, would create a new people, with a new heart and spirit of obedience (Ezek. 36:26-27). God would raise up for himself a folk that faithfully acknowledged his rule (Jer. 31:31-34; Ezek. 37:1-14). This new community, then, would become the germ cell of his universal gathering of all peoples (Isa. 2:2-4), the congregation of peace and unity, in which sin's ancient divisions were healed (Ezek. 37:15-23). With this new community God himself would dwell forever in love (Ezek. 37:24-28), pouring out upon it his abundant life (Ezek. 47:1-12). God would do these things, the prophets proclaimed, because he was indeed the Lord and therefore could not be deterred from bringing his purpose for life to fulfillment (Isa. 55:10-11).

It remained for God to accomplish those things which he promised through the words of his prophets. And in Jesus Christ his word became truly flesh—reality! By sending his Son, God began to turn his promise into fulfillment, his announced goal for the life of man into an accomplished fact.

We can trace the beginning of the fulfillment in the story of Jesus of Nazareth: his constant refusal to be ruled by other than the will of God, despite the charge of *scandalous lawbreaker* leveled against him by the pious; his complete renunciation of his own judgments and desires, even in the face of death, despite the fact that it had always seemed better to avoid the cross and its torture (cf. Mark 8:31-33; 14:36, 47-52, 66-72); his unshakable trust that in the midst of his suffering God was at work as the Lord and would bring out of evil and apparent defeat the victory of his kingship (Luke 23:46). Jesus Christ, in his life and death, refused to become a rebel, not against man whom he knew had no business playing ruler, but against his God whom he knew to be the real Lord over life.

The actions and faith of Christ were vindicated on that first day of the week, when God raised him from the dead to triumph over all the forces of evil to which man's sin had subjected him. Death, darkness, sin, suffering—none of these could bind him, and in the power of God the King he burst free from their shackles into new life. In Jesus Christ we see the lordship of God made clear. We see the One who perfectly trusted that God was in charge of life. We see God confirming that trust by the victory over the grave. In the life, death, and resurrection of his Son God clearly rules. It is in Christ's person and with his appearance, that God fully reveals his kingship.

God had wanted to make clear his rule through the medium of his people Israel. To accomplish his purpose he finally sent his own Son to fulfill Israel's role. Becoming a son of Israel, God's Son did what Israel was supposed to do, holding fast the faith which Israel was supposed to hold. God had promised Israel that her witness to his lordship would draw all men into her community of faith. When Jesus Christ was lifted up, he began to draw all men to himself (John 12:32).

So it is that in Jesus Christ there begins a new community, a new Israel which in belief and deed acknowledges the lordship of God. It is made up of all those who in Jesus Christ have come to see God's victorious and saving work, all those who commit their lives into the hands of the God of Jesus. It is not a people, therefore, which attempts to maintain its own self-righteousness and perfection. Rather, it looks to Christ for forgiveness and healing every day of its existence. It is not a folk which claims to know the way to live and think. Instead, it turns its ears to God to listen to his will, spoken through his Word. It is not skillfully wise or versed in carving out spheres of influence. Rather, it expectantly waits for the coming of the kingdom of God over all the earth. God's lordship! That is what Jesus Christ revealed on earth! And the people who share in Jesus Christ live under the rule of his Lord. The King alone saves, the King alone guides, the King alone finally conquers all. The people of God in Jesus Christ live by those facts.

The new community in Christ is not limited, therefore, by sin's ancient divisions. It includes every person who acknowledges the lordship of God in his Son. It transcends every boundary of race and nationality and language, healing Babel's chaos and disunity with its fellowship of common service to God. It takes up the broken ties of brotherhood and replaces jealousy and vengeance with love, which comes from the knowledge that in Jesus Christ all are judged and forgiven. It bestows upon the relationship of marriage a new oneness beyond sexuality and self-will. Male and female are bound together by the Lord' desire for their unity, and guided in their common path by a will transcending their own. The rule of God, known in Jesus Christ, heals the divisions of those who live under it. All who live in Christ are bound together by their common trust in the lordship of God and by the ruling action of God through Christ which alone redeems and sustains and guides them.

In other words, the community of God in Jesus Christ receives its life from God. It has no ties except the unity given it by the lordship of its Ruler. It has no purpose except to witness to that lordship. It has no goal except the inclusion of all men in its circle. But the life thus given God's new community is eternal and ever abundant, because it comes from the God who in Jesus Christ has won the victory over evil and the grave. Life from God is not destroyed by suffering or sin or death. The passing of any one member of the community cannot destroy his ties with either God or his fellows. And the work of every member of the community is given new meaning and purpose, as contributing to the total witness of the group to God's lordship over it. In the new people of God, begun in Jesus Christ, God gives the answer to the sinful divisions of men in the world. Out of chaos and disunity and destruction he brings order and fellowship and life. This was God's goal for his world. He began its fulfillment in Jesus Christ. Through Jesus Christ he continues to work until all is brought to perfection.

It is to the life of this new community, then, that we "saints in

Christ Jesus" are called. It is to live as members of the new people of God that we are set apart by our Lord. God has not forgiven you and me simply for our own sakes. He has not received us into his courts to give us a "spiritual experience," to make us "real persons," or to transform us into "Christian personalities." The development only of our individual selves is not the goal of his working. He has marked us out for the special function of living the life of the new community. Moreover, he has accomplished this deed not with a Savior out of the blue, but in Jesus Christ, who is the perfection and fulfillment of the long history of Israel. God's Son comes into the world to begin the New Israel of God. It is for the life of the New Israel that you and I are set apart.

Clearly, therefore, our sainthood in Christ means not only that we are free—free from all the pious legalism by which others would try to make us "religious." Our sainthood means also that we are responsible—responsible to God for living the life of his new people of faith. And this fact has definite implications for the bases of our religion.

3.

To live as members of the new community of God means to live in trust of God's lordship. But before we can do so, we have to be very clear about the nature of trust. In the first place, trust is not static belief. It is growing certainty, which is practiced and deepened every day in ever new and varying circumstances. Our trust is manifested, not in our acceptance of dogmas, but in our relations with our fellows and our world. Our trust is growing, not if it is merely a private conviction, but insofar as we learn to make decisions on the basis of it. This was the fact which Paul carefully pointed out to those immoral saints in his churches: that their sainthood in Christ had no meaning except it increasingly bore fruit in the life of God's community. Our trust, wrote Paul, is to become like the trust of Christ, and our trust is to grow, in decision and practice, until it grows up into the measure of the fullness of the stature of Christ's trust in his Father (cf. Eph. 4:13-16).

Secondly, we must realize that our trust can never grow except it be based upon a real knowledge of God. One of our more popular women authors once wrote in her enthusiasm, "Oh, that we all might love the Lord!" She then devoted one hundred pages to urging us toward that goal. But I ask you, how can we possibly love God if we do not know him? How can we learn to trust the Lord if we have no idea of his character and acts? We have to know whom it is we believe before faith is possible—know him in such a way that it alters the total outlook and course of our life. We have to know God, says the prophet Hosea, as a wife knows her husband. It is only when our knowledge of the Lord becomes that intimate that we will be willing to trust him with our lives.

It is for this reason that this little book in itself cannot help you grow in trust. And it is for this reason that I am wary of many "religious" books in general, especially those which claim to be devotional and inspirational guides. Such religious guides may be helpful in pointing the way, but as we use such books, we should keep two things in mind.

First of all, no book can present us with the person of God himself. Only God can do that. Only God, in his mercy, can reveal himself to us. And it is God upon whom we are called to rely. We cannot learn to know our Lord only by hearing second-hand descriptions of him. And this is true, not because God can be known only in some rapturous firsthand mystical experience of his presence, but because no secondhand description ever conveys the full range and authoritative lordship of his person. The God of the Bible has decisively revealed himself as Lord by a long series of particular acts in man's history, and unless those acts are known and understood, God's person is not made clear to us. Some religious books relate a few of the acts and their meaning, but it is safe to say that none tell the whole story. Thus, to know our God, we cannot rely on devotional and inspirational writings alone. We have to deal with the actual history in which God reveals himself.

Second, as in all areas of the Christian life, we must learn to be discriminating with regard to the religious "helps" we use. Far too often, devotional and inspirational guides ignore the history of God's acts altogether. Many of them simply go their own way, constructing a picture of God as their authors wish he might be. The result is a portrayal of a deity who does not, in fact, exist and who, if he did exist, would not deserve the name of God. The human mind can spin out marvelous theories in the religious realm. But such theories are totally worthless unless they conform to reality. We must choose and use religious helps which know the actual God of the Bible.

In the same manner, we must realize that we are not necessarily obeying God's will simply by adopting someone else's religious regime. I have read many volumes on how to pray. Some are helpful; some are not. But I have come to mistrust women speakers and circles who tell me what I *must* do to be "religious." Especially do I recoil from those religious books for women which start out by telling me to relax, because I have yet to find in the Word of God a call to "take it easy." I always have to ask myself, when confronted with such books and speakers, if they are actually asking me to respond to *God*. And do their recommended religious exercises have anything at all to do with that life of trust which God himself requires of me? We women, who are barraged with religious propaganda these days, have to keep our object very clearly in mind: to trust in God the Lord and not in a construction of man. We therefore have to learn to be theologically discriminating in our choice of religious guides.

At the same time, we have to remember that we are called to trust *within a community*. And in this connection, my wary nature comes to the fore again. On every side, I am met by people promising to help or to save me as an individual. But again, I always have to ask, Is this the life to which we are called? Are we not rather commanded by God to live the life of a new *people* of faith? How, then, can my restoration take place outside of such a context? I know for a fact that "Jesus Christ saves," as the billboards insistently announce. But I also know that the life of salvation must be life in a fellowship.

In short, in the light of our freedom and responsibility as "saints in Jesus Christ," I reject many current religious offerings. I reject every book and speaker which claims to be a substitute for God himself. I reject every religious discipline which would substitute man's way for God's will. And I reject every call to faith which knows nothing of *the Church*, by which I mean not a denomination or sect, but the new community established in Jesus Christ. It is to trust in the Lordship of God that we "saints in Christ" are called, and we dare not try to replace that lordship with disciplines and devices of our own making. Here, as always, we must be able to discern the helpful guide from the harmful. And if we have a real knowledge of God himself, that knowledge will aid us in such discernment. Indeed, a real knowledge of God will often dictate its own response and devotion. And only as we come to know the Lord himself will our trust, as members of his new community, assuredly deepen and grow.

The crucial question is, therefore, from where do we have our knowledge of God? And the answer is that we can know our God only through his own self-revelation. We can know him only as he has made himself known in his own words and acts, and the record of those is contained in and mediated through the history in the Bible. If we want to live the life of trust, we must come to know God through the Scriptures much more adequately than we have ever known him before. It is through the Scriptures' words that we are confronted with the person and Word of the living Lord.

This is not to say that God is limited to a book, by which I mean that he acts in our lives in many other ways than through the medium of the *written* word. Indeed, anyone who has understood the Bible would not dream of limiting God, for the Bible itself portrays him sweeping through history in sovereign might and love. We have only to know the account of his dealings with the empires of the ancient Middle East to realize that the Lord cannot be bound or encompassed within any limits by man.

Furthermore, I am not saying that the Bible is infallible. Its sentences are not to be read as the absolute, verbal dictations of God, and its words are not to be taken as literalistically holy and unchangeable in themselves. The Bible is a human product, full of human errors. Some portions of the Hebrew text of the Old Testament, for example, are so corrupted by scribal errors and glosses that they are unreadable. Throughout, the Bible evidences several different layers of tradition and experience and faith. And its history as a whole has been reworked and reinterpreted many different times, from many different viewpoints, by many different authors, in many different places.

Nevertheless, the Bible as it has come down to us from the hands of storytellers and scribes and churchmen preserves a remarkably unified witness to unique events, preserved in no other place. It witnesses to the words and acts of God by which he revealed himself in the life of man. And it continues to be the authoritative medium of that revelation. To trust God's lordship, therefore, we have got to know and study the Bible, much more adequately and thoroughly than we have ever done before, for it is only through the Scriptures' witness that we can come to know whom we believe.

As we enter by study into those events which are mediated to us through the biblical story, God's revealed person and will slowly become clear to us. We begin to learn what God did on behalf of the old Israel. Slowly we begin to realize that he is doing the same things for us, his new Israel, in his Son Jesus Christ. We learn a little more from the Bible, each time we study it, of how the Lord expects his people Israel to live together and with him. We enter into centuries of time in which prophets and apostles and God's Son himself show us what God is doing. And on the basis of the Word of God, we begin to be aware of God's continuing actions, both within his new community and without in all of life.

Because the Word of God is alive and influential, working its effects in our hearts and minds and actions, slowly our trust begins to grow. Slowly we begin to understand, in a way that makes a difference, the incredible faithfulness and mercy of this God of Israel. Slowly we come to realize that his is a power which undergirds our total existence. Slowly we perceive his rule, governing every moment of time. And our understanding and realization and perception are not theoretical or secondhand. They are based on our confrontation and real knowledge of the Lord, as he meets us through the Scriptures.

It is for this reason that the Bible has always been considered the final authority in Protestantism: its witness presents us not with dogmas and dead-letter rules, but with the living action and presence of the Lord himself, who is the Ruler of all of life. When we experience the actions of God, as they are mediated to us through the Scriptures, all other authorities and rules for life are seen to be idolatrous imitations. Our trust turns toward the Lord of power and love, who has accepted and forgiven us and who, we begin to realize, is able to do all things. More and more we come to give the whole of our existence, and that of our fellows, into his hands.

It is in this way that we grow in the Christian life, responding ever more fully and certainly, in ever-new situations of community, to the God whom we come to know more and more through the Scriptures. Prayer, in such a manner of life, is not an artificial discipline, but the natural response to the person of God whom we find ever more certainly with us. Sacrifice and disciplined devotion are not acts set apart, but responses made in the context of growing trust and knowledge of the Lord. Finally, love for God becomes the fruit of such a life, for the trusting believer comes to a time when he knows with unshakable certainty, that the God who gives and guides his life in Christ is, above all others, lovable!

At the center of the new community of God there must be the Word of God, the story of the Old and New Testaments through which God reveals himself. Thus to trust, to grow, to be the new people of faith, the church must hear the Word, proclaimed in reading and sacrament, and interpreted in the sermon. But at the same time, every individual member of the church, to live up to his responsibility, must singly and together with others, consistently read and study the Scriptures.

The Bible is a very old book. Some of its traditions are three thousand years old, and there is no history so old which can be understood in a casual reading. It takes work to understand the Bible. It takes scholarly help. And there are now easily available to every woman in the United States good commentaries and guides to Bible study.[8] These commentaries and guides should be used and reused, daily and continually.

Moreover, despite its diversity, the Bible contains a unified story. No mere study of one book or even of one testament will bring its full revelation to light. There is little point in reading a random

[8] Three series of commentaries which the lay woman will find helpful are: *The Interpreter's Bible* (12 vols.; Nashville: Abingdon Press, 1951-57); *The Layman's Bible Commentary* (25 vols.; Richmond: John Knox Press, 1960-64); *Westminster Guides to the Bible* (9 vols.; Philadelphia: The Westminster Press, 1959-62). See also Suggested Helps for Bible Study, p. 153.

Bible verse each day. There is only limited value in memorizing passages out of their context. The Bible must be read and studied, patiently and consistently, with such faithfulness to its total intent, that its unified witness is grasped.

Starting as so many of us do with such a meager knowledge of the Scriptures, it seems an almost impossible task to become acquainted with the total Bible. It is much easier to read the latest religious novels, to have our religion secondhand from little books such as this, to ride the comfortable crest of the newest popular religion, or to gather bits and snippets of the Word from women's meetings and discussions. But if we avoid our responsibility as saints in Jesus Christ, if we never learn to know our God through the Scriptures as he has revealed himself in man's life and time, if we never grow in our trust of his lordship over his people, then surely we will wander away from his life-giving spring, like senseless travelers in a desert, refusing an oasis' water. God has accepted us and made us saints in his Son. God offers us his living water, his life in all its eternal abundance and fructifying power (cf. John 4:13-14; Ezek. 47:1-12; Ps. 1:3). He has done everything possible to insure that we may live, in knowledge and trust and obedience to him, as members of his new community. Now his invitation is for us to accept his life, which is mediated through the Word:

> Ho, every one who thirsts,
> come to the waters (Isa. 55:1).

CHAPTER III
LOSING GOD THROUGH NATURE

Among all of the world's Christians, there is probably no group more lost in natural religion today than are middle-class American females. Part and parcel of their religious faith is the belief that God is revealed through his creation. All over the nation, women figuratively or literally "lift up their eyes unto the hills," in the mistaken certainty that through nature's wonders they will be granted knowledge of the Lord.[1] They find God revealed in the

---

[1] Actually, many women misinterpret this well-known line from Ps. 121. The correct reading and punctuation from the original Hebrew are:

> I lift up my eyes to the hills.
> From whence does my help come?
> My help comes from the Lord,
> who made heaven and earth.

In the thought of the psalmist the hills are a source of danger, either because they hide lurking robber bands or because they are the site of idolatrous Canaanite worship at the "high places." The comfort of the psalmist is that God is the Lord and Creator, above and in control of the created world.

beauty of lakes and trees. The orderliness of the universe is the "proof" of his existence. The awesomeness of natural wonders makes him seem very near. Thus women turn to the natural world to find their God and to increase their knowledge of him, unaware that they have thereby become idolaters from the standpoint of the biblical faith. It is not that women worship nature itself. It is that they believe they can commune with God through nature and that nature can furnish them with true knowledge of their Lord. In short, nature is viewed by them as a medium of revelation.

On the simplest level, many women believe that God is literally revealed "in" nature. The beauty, the harmony, the awesomeness, and power of natural wonders reflect the divine presence. Contemplating Niagara's roar or the thrush's song in a silent wood, the women feel met by an inexplicable wonder which they attribute to divinity. In such pantheistic worship they are, of course, imitating most primitive religions; for every people from the ancient Babylonians to the Romans saw the gods revealed in nature's processes and powers. But unlike that of some primitives, the modern female's pantheism is not due to an inability to explain nature. Rather, it stems from the universal experience of "another dimension" permeating reality. To this dimension thousands of females assign the name of God, and their goal is then to become "at one" or harmoniously unified with it. In fact, this is what many women mean when they talk of a "spiritual experience"—the experience of a "presence" in nature and the entrance into a oneness with it.

On a more rationalistic level, many women speak of God as being revealed "through" nature. For them, the orderliness and design of the world point to a Wisdom behind them. The marvelous mechanisms of the human body, the color lavished even on an insect, the ordered procession of millions of stars across the span of the heavens—these point to a Creator's hand which has fashioned them all. The women join in the song of the psalmist:

74

The heavens are telling the glory of God;
and the firmament proclaims his handiwork (Ps. 19:1).

For such women, the most certain proofs of the existence of God
are these evidences of his handiwork. In this belief they are joined
by many modern scientists, who win the approval of these female
naturalists, by stating that science has led them to what they consider the basic conclusion of faith: there must be a God after all.
As does every other non-Christian religion in the world, with the
exception of Judaism and its derivative Islam, this naturalistic type
of religion starts with the phenomena of the universe. From the
created world it then deduces the existence and character of God.

On the most sophisticated level, there is also a small group
of women who talk about God "under" nature. These are women,
who from contemporary theological discussions, and from the
popular book *Honest to God*,[2] have picked up the jargon of
"depth": God is the depth of nature, "the Ground of being," or "Being itself." Someone once humorously labeled this type of talk "base-
ment theology." Its point is that it identifies God with the principle
or power of all existence. The reality, the life, which underlies
nature, man, and the universe are given the name of God. God is
that which makes everything able simply "to be." He is met in all
phenomena as the ultimate Ground of existence. Indeed, he is the
Being itself of existence. Without God there would "be" simply
nothing at all. Because God "is," there is instead, something and
not nothing. The point of such depth religion, then, is to share in
the Being of God, and thus to be delivered from the anxiety and
nothingness of nonbeing and its destruction. God as Being per-
meates the life of all. Man's task is to become aware and one with
the ultimate depth sustaining his existence.

Because many women are adherents of one or another forms or

[2] J. A. T. Robinson (Philadelphia: The Westminster Press, 1963).

combinations of these natural religions, they therefore usually take one of two views toward the biblical faith. Either they syncretistically combine their natural religion with a vague acceptance of the basic biblical position, or more often they practically, if not theoretically, deny the uniqueness of the biblical Word altogether. "Why," is their unspoken question, "should we seek God only through the biblical history? After all, God reveals himself in the whole of his creation. His revelation of himself in Jesus Christ is one avenue to his person, to be sure. But the same God can also be known through his presence and works in the world of nature."

Indeed, in recent times, women have added a new facet to what the Bible would term their baalism (that is, the worship of God as *revealed through* the created world). Because most American women now are residents of cities and suburbs, separated from the great out-of-doors, they have in increasing numbers begun to believe that God is revealed through any form of beauty or order. To their way of thinking "religion and the arts" have become inseparable, and God can be found through music and painting, ballet and sculpture and architecture.

Now let me say immediately that the creative arts have an indispensable part to play in the Christian religion. They can brilliantly portray the human situation. They can, as they often do, point to the biblical history through which God has in fact revealed himself. But often in modern forms of baalism, the arts themselves are viewed as mediums of revelation. The biblical history is completely bypassed, and the artist's work in itself is viewed as a window opening to the divine.

Indeed, in this type of natural religion, any medium which expresses "truth" in any form is considered by many women somehow to express the truth of God. Pushed to its furtherest extreme, this view holds that $2 \times 2 = 4$ is an expression of the divine, because all truth or beauty or order is considered an expression of the life of God. The knowledge of God is mediated through every facet of the created world. It seems senseless to those holding such views to limit God's revelation of himself to the medium of the biblical history.

It is not surprising that modern American women persist in such beliefs. (And through all of the changes in the church's life in America, no faith has been so persistent as baalism.) Women, despite their participation in the technological age of the twentieth century, always retain an affinity for the unending cycle of nature. It is given to them to share in the mystery of fecundity and birth. They know intimately the pangs of that power that forces their infant, bloodily gasping, into life. They watch and adjust to their child's innate rhythm of suckling and sleep and suckling. They quietly marvel at the unseen order that leads him inalterably from infanthood to adolescence. Through it all, they tremulously sense the dissonance that death could bring, if laughter and tears and hurts and triumphs were silenced by the end's sudden stillness. Life takes on a wondrous divinity for women who are mothers, and they hug it close, in all its fragility, and endue it with ultimate importance. It is not strange for a mother to call nature by the name of God. Its powers and cycles and orders give the basic facts to her life.

It is also not surprising that modern women, who have been forced by their role in society to seek meaning for their lives in cultural and artistic pursuits, sometimes tend to absolutize the fruits of those pursuits. When it is music and painting and home decorating that provide a woman with her sense of achievement and purpose, she tends to ascribe to their beauty and form ultimate worth and purpose. She feels met in them by truth to which she can be committed. She feels responsible for expressing that truth in her home and surroundings. Art becomes for such a woman a

77

window opening to the ultimate, her means of entrance into divine purpose and verity.

That which is surprising about the modern woman's baalism is the fact that she is frequently encouraged and nurtured in it by her church. It is the supposed body of Christ itself which is talking more and more in present-day America about "religion and the arts." It is the church which exploits the statements of those scientists who think to confirm the existence of God. It is the church which frequently at Eastertime links the resurrection of Christ with the revival of all life in the springtime. And it is the church which time and again, in its retreats and sunrise services and prayers about nature's revelations, gives the impression that God can be known through the wonders of his creation.

Actually, no impression could be more erroneous, from the standpoint of the biblical faith. The Bible does, to be sure, praise God's works in the world of nature, just as we should praise them. And those works are evidences of God's inestimable wisdom and majesty and power. In the poetry and liturgies of the Bible, God has created the light (Gen. 1:3) and covered himself with it like a garment (Ps. 104:2). The heavens are his tent, the oceans lap the foundations of his chambers (Ps. 104:2-3). He uses the clouds for his chariot, the winds are his errand boys (Ps. 104:3-4). His voice echoes in the thunderstorm (Ps. 29). The stars are all there because he has counted them (Isa. 40:26). The sun and the moon are the calendar he has set in the heavens (Gen. 1:14-16; Ps. 104:19).

> O Lord, how manifold are thy works!
> In wisdom hast thou made them all (Ps. 104:24).

Such is the biblical affirmation of the goodness of God's creation (cf. Gen. 1:31). The universe shows forth the power and wisdom of its Creator.

Yet it is significant in the Bible that such natural religion is never allowed to stand alone. Everywhere God's revelation of himself in nature is subordinated to the revelation of himself through his acts in the history of Israel. For example, a passage like Neh. 9:6 ff. praises God as Creator, but it immediately goes on to talk of Abraham and the exodus and Sinai. Psalm 29 gives the most vivid description of God's manifestations in a thunderstorm over the Mediterranean. But its climax emphasizes the lordship of God over his historical congregation on Zion. The author of Psalm 19 hears "the heavens . . . telling the glory of God" (v. 1), but it is the law given to Moses, not the witness of the heavens, which revives his soul (v. 7), and he prays not to a God of nature, but to *one who has acted to redeem him* (v. 14).

Always the Bible's emphasis is on God's acts in relation to men. It is those acts which furnish Israel with her essential knowledge of her Lord. The exodus, the wilderness wanderings, the gift of the land, the law and the prophets, finally the life, death, and resurrection of Jesus Christ—these are the mediums God uses in the Bible to reveal himself to his people.

Indeed, in Israel's earliest confessions of faith (Deut. 6:20-23; 26:5-9; Josh. 24:2-13), God's relations with nature are not even mentioned. The doctrine of God as Creator is developed only later on the basis of Israel's earlier historical experiences of God as Redeemer and Judge.[3] Because God has the power to deliver her from Egypt, for example, Israel concludes that his is the ultimate power which has created the world and which will at the end of time bring creation to perfection (cf. Isa. 51:9-11). In fact, to the prophets' way of thinking, it is this which distinguishes the God of Israel from every other god of nature—the fact that he has the power to save his people and to bring his purpose to fulfillment (Isa. 46). Only the God who can redeem and fulfill can be Lord of

---

[3] Cf. Ps. 78, which has no doctrine of creation, with the later Ps. 136.

the creation (Isa. 45). Nature gods who cannot act in history are mocked by the prophets as nonentities (Isa. 44:9-20; Jer. 2:5; 10:1-10; I Kings 18:17-40). Other religions may start with the creation and deduce God from it. The Bible starts with God's relations with man, namely Israel, and concludes that he must be the Creator.

Thus to maintain that the God of the Bible can be known through his creation is patently false to the Bible's witness. That witness never pretends to find in the creation the full revelation of God. It always makes God's revelation of himself in the natural world subordinate to and dependent upon his revelation of himself in the history of Israel.

In fact, the Bible sees one result of natural religion divorced from historical: worship of God through nature leads finally to idolatry (cf. Rom. 1:18-25). Men come to worship and serve the creature rather than the Creator (Rom. 1:25). The truths of the created world —of art or mathematics or form—come to be accepted as truths about God.

The Bible therefore fights against baalism, in every period of Israel's history, with all of the power at its disposal. And the second of the Ten Commandments is formulated specifically to combat every form of natural religion: "You shall not make yourself a graven image, or any likeness of anything that is in heaven above, or that is in the earth beneath, or that is in the water under the earth; you shall not bow down to them or serve them" (Exod. 20:4-5; cf. Deut. 5:8-9). We women of the modern world usually interpret this command to apply only to ancient idols and graven images, and thus we consider it largely irrelevant to our present life. But the mere prohibition of images was not at all the sole purpose of the command. It was designed to legislate against nature worship in every form.

Despite our crude estimation of primitive idol worship, ancient man rarely considered an image to *contain* his god. Rather, the image was a transparent symbol, *through which* his God was revealed. It pointed beyond itself to the presence of the divine. Thus anything could be an image or idol for the ancients—stones, trees, groves, plain wooden poles. The point was that they were places or things in the created world, at which or through which the divine became known to man.

This is the understanding of God and his worship which the second commandment fights: the view that God is to be known or worshiped through anything in all creation. Nothing that is in heaven above, that is in the earth, or that is in the water, in short *nothing in all the created world is adequate to reveal God*—and that includes all art and form, all created beauty and truth. The God of the Bible makes himself known to man only by his own acts and words in man's life. When we seek him through other than his self-revelation, we break his commandment for us.

1.

Now some of the reasoning behind the Bible's antagonism to baalism is immediately apparent. For it is quite clear that nature and art, no matter how beautiful or majestic in their order, do not reveal that God loves and judges, fights and forgives, to make himself a people. Nor do they tell that he sent his Son finally to fulfill his purpose of community. Without God's acts in the history of Israel, we would know nothing of his redemption, nothing of his power to rule men, nothing of his purpose.

Indeed, without God's acts through his chosen people, we would have only the most limited inkling of his love, for the beauty and order of creation shield behind them an awful realm of violence and destruction. There is in the most peaceful wood a fight for existence going on, between big tree and little tree to find a place in the sun,

81

between predator and prey to quiet the pangs of hunger. There is in every nook of nature a struggle for survival, and if it is the medium of the revelation of the divine, then its lesson is simply that the big gods eat the little ones. Those who find God revealed only through his creation must ignore the flood, the drought, the earthquake, or else they must inevitably conclude that God's purpose is death as much as life. In the same manner, if God is revealed only through man in a natural state, then God is the Creator not only of Jesus, but also of the hatred which drove the nails into Jesus' hands. And the world will never be, and was not intended to be, any different than it is today. Natural revelation, apart from the Word, gives forth a picture of a Creator as demonic as he is divine, and the self-giving sacrifice of the cross has no place at all in it.

This would be reason enough to reject the idolatry of baalism. But the Bible's antagonism to natural religion goes even deeper than this. It sees Baal and the Lord of Israel to be irreconcilable opponents, because it knows that baalism in all its forms is a denial of the lordship of God.

For example, baalism is a denial of God's sovereign independence, and if God is known only through the medium of creation, we can never know that he is free and above creation as its ruling Lord. We may find God "in" nature, but nature is only transitory and the "eternal hills," on closer inspection, are found not to be eternal at all. Does God, too, then age and pass like the creation which is supposed to reveal him? Is he slowly dying away as some astronomers tell us our galaxy is dying? [4]

In the evidence that creation gives there is no reassuring answer to these questions. But the Word of God is quite definite about the eternity of the Lord:

[4] Loren C. Eiseley, "Man: The Lethal Factor," in *The Key Reporter*, XXVIII (Spring, 1963), 4.

Of old thou didst lay the foundation of the earth,
and the heavens are the work of thy hands.
They will perish, but thou dost endure;
they will all wear out like a garment.
Thou changest them like raiment, and they pass way;
but thou art the same, and thy years have no end
(Ps. 102:25-27).

In the same manner, we may think God is revealed "through" the wonders of his creation. But what if those wonders are suddenly blackened and covered by the dust of an atomic holocaust? Is God, then, forever lost to us, and fellowship with him obliterated? A prominent Boston rabbi wrote some time ago:

If God could change the past or abrogate the law of gravity or cause it to rain in the absence of clouds, I could no longer believe in God because the principle of organization and causality and integration which men have perceived in nature would no longer be there.[5]

But such a view expresses a feeble faith when compared with the certainty of Israel:

God is our refuge and strength,
a very present help in trouble.
Therefore we will not fear though the earth should change,
though the mountains shake in the heart of the sea (Ps. 46:1-2).

In other words, in the faith of the Bible, even if a catastrophe overtakes the creation, even if the world slips from its very axis or a hydrogen fission reduces us to ashes, we know with certainty that we are not thereby separated from the love of God. The prophet Jeremiah speaks of the reversal of the whole creative process (Jer. 4:23-26), but above it all, in sovereign majesty, there remains for

[5] Rabbi Roland B. Gittelsohn of Boston, "Have We Outgrown God," in *Saturday Review*, September 16, 1961.

him God the Lord. And because God remains, the psalmist looks forward to an eternal fellowship with him, when flesh and everything on this earth have passed away forever:

> I am continually with thee;
> thou dost hold my right hand.
> Thou dost guide me with thy counsel,
> and afterward thou wilt receive me to glory.
> Whom have I in heaven but thee?
> And there is nothing upon earth that I desire besides thee.
> My flesh and my heart may fail,
> but God is the strength of my heart and my portion for ever (Ps. 73:23-26).

Baalism does not inspire such certainty. We may think to find God "under" all that is, as the Being of everything that shares in creation's existence. But what does that mean when we sit sorrowing and dumb before the corpse of a loved one? Where is the Being that sustains the life in that pale and motionless body? Does anything in all creation tell us that death is not final and that the passage of time will not bear every friend and relative away forever? Or does it take the Word of God and a risen Lord to make us know that the grave has no victory and that death has lost its sting? The god of nature is singularly impotent as a lord over life and death.

In other words, it is only as God is independent of his creation, as the Lord over it, that we have assurance of his free power to preserve our lives in an eternal community. The Second Isaiah knows this very well:

> Lift up your eyes to the heavens,
> and look at the earth beneath;
> for the heavens will vanish like smoke,

> the earth wear out like a garment,
> and they who dwell in it will die like gnats;
> but my salvation will be for ever,
> and my deliverance will never be ended (Isa. 51:6).

There is nothing in the religion of baalism which gives such a revelation. To natural religion, God is "in," "through," or "under" his creation, inseparably connected with it. But in the revelation of the Word, God is independent of his world:

> Lord, thou hast been our dwelling place
> in all generations.
> Before the mountains were brought forth,
> or ever thou hadst formed the earth and the world
> from everlasting to everlasting thou art God
>
> (Ps. 90:1-2).

Before there ever were being or truth or form as we know them on this planet, before there ever were nature or a world or a whole universe of galaxies, there was God who in lordly might created them all. And after they have all disappeared, there will still be God (cf. Mal. 3:6). It is no wonder that the prophet Isaiah calls the deities of nature by the name of "nothings" (*elilim* in the Hebrew, Isa. 2:8, 18; 10:10; 19:3), for so they are in comparison with the eternal King who has revealed himself through his people Israel. That King is known only through his Word, and indeed, it is precisely the biblical doctrine of the Word which most clearly expresses God's sovereign independence.

In both the Old and New Testaments, God is said to have created all things by his Word (Gen. 1; John 1:1-3). And this statement is a conscious witness to God's lordship over his handiwork. The Bible is saying that there is a separation and a difference between

God and his world. That is, between us and God, between creation and Creator, there stands the Word of God: the creation is not an extension of the life of God; God is not contained in any way in any part of his creation, not even in a divine spark within the soul of man. Rather, God acts in creation through the medium of his Word. For example, God *says,* "Let there be light," and there is light (Gen. 1:3). And God is to be known, then, by his creatures, through the medium of the Word. Only through his Word, made flesh in Jesus Christ, do we come to know the Creator as he really reveals himself, namely as the everlasting, independent Lord who rules and saves us, though heaven and earth pass away.

2.

To go further, worship of God through the medium of his creation is a denial of his purpose, a denial of the fact that as the Lord he has a goal for his universe and man.

It is characteristic of nature that it moves in cycles or spirals, in a seemingly endless repetition of birth and life and death. Occasionally, through the processes of evolution, new forms of life are introduced. But these too are then absorbed in the vast circle of repetition, reproducing and passing away over millennia of time, reappearing, growing, fading in time's tedious succession.

Women who have given any thought to the ways of their existence know, perhaps better than men, the endless turning of nature's wheel. After all, they are the wombs of human life, constantly bearing and bringing forth the succession of generations. And given a little objective thought, we women are forced to ask, "Why? Why this cyclic repetition of birth and growth and death? Why am I bringing forth children and raising them painstakingly, in order that they in turn can raise more children, who in turn will raise still more? Why this endless repetition of the generations of mankind? To what goal is it leading? What is the purpose of it all?"

These questions become even more poignant for a woman while her children are young. For in her children she senses so well the great pathos with which our cycle of life is permeated. It is so full of feeling! The embarrassment of a little child or his hurts at the hands of his playmates; his joy in a moment of acceptance or his anticipation of a tomorrow; his fear of anger or his sudden apprehensiveness over some discord: these emotions all lie exposed and naked to a mother who cares for a child. And we find ourselves asking why, if they age and pass, are they so important to life? And why does every new generation of children relive them all, in their tenderness and pain and joy? Why is it given to the children of men to feel and to feel and to feel, in a seemingly ever recurring, never ceasing, endless monotony of emotion?

Even a woman's life as a housewife involves her in the great cycle of nature, for her tasks are dictated by that ceaseless round of "cold and heat, summer and winter, day and night" (Gen. 8:22), each with their specific demands. Her work becomes largely a matter of repeatedly meeting the needs imposed on us by nature. She washes and mends, cleans and arranges, prepares and serves to meet our creaturely requirements. And her tasks follow their pattern as regularly as does one day the next. It is no wonder that women often feel that they are not getting anywhere. Their life is basically made up of going around in a circle, of doing the same things over and over again—tasks which their mothers have done in the years before, tasks which their children will repeat after they are gone.

In the experience of it all, modern women are not only led to ask why. They sometimes become filled with the weariness and meaninglessness that haunted the writer of Ecclesiastes (a writer whose views, incidentally, are completely different from those of the rest of the Scriptures):

What does man gain by all the toil
at which he toils under the sun?
A generation goes, and a generation comes,
but the earth remains for ever.
The sun rises and the sun goes down,
and hastens to the place where it rises.
The wind blows to the south,
and goes round to the north;
round and round goes the wind,
and on its circuits the wind returns.
All streams run to the sea,
but the sea is not full;
to the place where the streams flow,
there they flow again.
All things are full of weariness;
a man cannot utter it;
the eye is not satisfied with seeing,
nor the ear filled with hearing.
What has been is what will be,
and what has been done is what will be done;
and there is nothing new under the sun.
Is there a thing of which it is said,
"See, this is new"?
It has been already,
in the ages before us.
There is no remembrance of former things,
nor will there be any remembrance
of later things yet to happen
among those who come after (Eccl. 1:3-11).

Such, in truth, is the meaningless mood of many a modern woman, occupying her tiny spoke in the great revolving wheel of nature. She lives, she works, she bears, she dies, to be replaced by the next generation. And on and on and on rolls the wheel, toward no perceptible goal. Why, a woman must ask. To what purpose is it all?

The fact is that in the religion of nature there is no answer to these questions. Nature itself cannot furnish a reason for its ceaseless cycle. Like "ol' man river" in the song, "it just keeps rollin' along." It has no goal or terminus revealed in its repetitive revolutions. Similarly, a God who is tied to nature is as purposeless as the nature that reveals him, and even the additions of evolution's changes give no clue to his goal. Perhaps Creator and creation are both developing toward an ultimate perfection (for there are some philosophers, indeed, who hold that God himself is in or is identical with the process of becoming!) Perhaps, on the other hand, both nature and God are rolling on to a fiery *Goetterdaemmerung,* when the universe and the God it reveals will both disappear in smoke. It would seem a meaningless end to our years of pathos and plans and work. But the religion of Baal, for all its beauty, is not designed to give much assurance.

If in the middle of this ceaseless round, however, you place the Word of God, suddenly human life and the creation around it have a goal and a purpose and a meaning. No longer is the purpose of existence limited to nature's cycle. The purpose is given by the Creator of all life, who stands over it as its Lord. In the words of Second Isaiah,

> Who has measured the waters in the hollow of his hand
>   and marked off the heavens with a span,
> enclosed the dust of the earth in a measure
>   and weighed the mountains in scales
>   and the hills in a balance? (Isa. 40:12.)

The God of the Bible holds his creation in his hands! He is not contained in it. He stands outside of it and reigns over it (cf. Ps.

95:3-5). And because he is thus Lord of his creation, he is the one who gives nature and man their goal and purpose for being!

The Word is very plain. We are not participating as meaningless members in a great silly cycle of life and death. The meaning and purpose of our life are not to be found in nature at all. Rather, we are born, as unique individuals, into unique moments of time, for the purpose of participating in a community whose life is pleasing to God. The feelings we feel, the work we do, the plans we make and carry out are the arenas of the decisions we make to participate in that community or not. Every moment of our lives we decide to move with God's purpose or against it. And every decision thus made is new and unrepeatable. Our life is not an endless cycle of repetition. It is a movement toward or away from God's goal of community.

In the same manner, the life of nature is not an infinite spiral of dying and becoming. The God who rules as nature's Lord has a goal for its life, too. Far from being a medium adequate to reveal the life of the divine, the Bible tells us that nature too is disrupted and imperfect and filled with chaos by man's sin. In the poetry of Thomas Lovell Beddoes,

Nature's polluted,
There's man in every secret corner of her
Doing damned wicked deeds. Thou art, old world,
A hoary, atheistic, murdering star.

The thought is not much different from that of the prophet Jeremiah:

How long will the land mourn,
and the grass of every field wither?
For the wickedness of those who dwell in it

the beasts and the birds are swept away,
because men said, "He will not see our latter end"
(Jer. 12:4).

As Paul puts it, "The whole creation has been groaning in travail together until now" (Rom. 8:22), groaning with the futility and hopelessness of men in rebellion against God. I suppose I can make that clearest by pointing out that man, "doing damned wicked deeds," has the capacity now to detonate nuclear warheads of such destruction that the very springs themselves of nature's life could be dried up forevermore. But the Bible tells us it has always been that way, with Cain polluting the ground with the blood of his brother Abel (Gen. 4:10-12), and the land made a "desolation and a waste" by those trying to possess it (Ezek. 33:23-29). Man's sin has always had the effects of a "scorched earth policy" on God's good creation. And nature too "waits with eager longing for the revealing of the sons of God" (Rom. 8:19).

It is for this reason that the Bible's poetry portrays all creation shouting for joy, when God finally establishes his kingdom among men over all the earth:

> For you shall go out in joy,
>   and be led forth in peace;
> the mountains and the hills before you
>   shall break forth into singing,
>   and all the trees of the field shall clap their hands
>   (Isa. 55:12).

> Let the sea roar, and all that fills it;
>   the world and those who dwell in it!
> Let the floods clap their hands;
>   let the hills sing for joy together
> before the Lord, for he comes to rule the earth
>   (Ps. 98:7-9a).

THE FEMININE CRISIS IN CHRISTIAN FAITH

It is for this reason, too, that the prophets of the Bible borrow the language of mythology to picture the effects of the kingdom on nature:

> The wolf shall dwell with the lamb,
>   and the leopard shall lie down with the kid,
> and the calf and the lion and the fatling together,
>   and a little child shall lead them.
> The cow and the bear shall feed;
>   their young shall lie down together;
>   and the lion shall eat straw like the ox.
> The sucking child shall play over the hole of the asp,
>   and the weaned child shall put his hand on the
>   adder's den,[6]
> They shall not hurt or destroy
>   in all my holy mountain;
> for the earth shall be full of the knowledge of the Lord
>   as the waters cover the sea (Isa. 11:6-9).

The Bible is telling us, with this poetry, that nature now is corrupted and imperfect. But when the kingdom of God is established, nature will share in its redemption. In biblical faith, the created world does not reveal the purpose of God. Rather, it too is given its purpose and goal by the God who is beyond and above it.

3.

There is another objection to baalism, from the standpoint of the Bible. Baalism—the worship of God through the medium of creation—is a denial of God's lordship over man, a denial of the fact that we are responsible to him.

[6] Note that here the life and death struggle between woman and evil, as symbolized by the story of Eve and the serpent (Gen. 3:15), is portrayed as ended in the kingdom of God.

92

There is something very superficially soothing about a god of nature. Whatever the name by which we call Baal, he makes few demands upon us. Being itself, the soul of the world, the truth of beauty and form, a great life force, an ultimate one—all are completely impersonal. And as impersonal things or deities, these Baals have no will of their own. The only requirement they lay upon us is that we get lost in them. Like some bacchanalian spirit, they beckon us to shed our individuality, to lose our identity, and to float in their bottomless abysses of beauty. "Be yourselves," "return to nature," "become at one with the world"—these are the slogans that baalism holds temptingly before us. Its aim is to merge our souls with the great soul of nature, and thus to share in nature's supposedly divine life and truth and peace. Its goal is lovely, its way is broad, and all paths lead to fulfillment. We have only to lose ourselves in the all-encompassing one.

Over against such lovely nonsense, the real God of the Bible addresses us personally, as he addressed the prophet Ezekiel: "Son of man, stand upon your feet, and I will speak with you" (Ezek. 2:1). The command is not a general address to some disembodied soul, not a lovely truth available within all realms of truth. It is a Word, a concrete Word, spoken to me as an individual. And it requires that I, as a person, listen and respond to it. The Bible is full of such Words, and they all require our personal response:

You shall have no other gods before me (Exod. 20:3).

Hear, O Israel: The Lord our God is one Lord; and you shall love the Lord your God with all your heart, and with all your soul, and with all your might (Deut. 6:4-5).

Let justice roll down like waters,
and righteousness like an everflowing stream (Amos 5:24).

93

> For I tell you, unless your righteousness exceeds that of the scribes and Pharisees, you will never enter the kingdom of heaven.
>
> Love your enemies and pray for those who persecute you.
>
> If you love those who love you, what reward have you?
>
> Beware of practicing your piety before men in order to be seen by them.
>
> Do not lay up for yourselves treasure on earth.
>
> Do not be anxious about your life.
>
> Judge not, that you be not judged.
>
> Beware of false prophets. (Matt. 5-7, *passim*).
>
> If any man would come after me, let him deny himself and take up his cross and follow me (Mark 8:34).
>
> I am the resurrection and the life (John 11:25).

You cannot escape the demands and claims of Words such as these. Either you decide to act upon them or you reject their speaker and his will. But as is not the case in the religion of nature, you are called to make a decision. That decision belongs to you, as a fully responsible person, called to decide to obey or not to obey your God. You are not lost in the crowd before the God of the Bible. You are not a nameless nonentity, blurred into nature's soul. You are God's unique creation, created to respond to him. And only you as a responsible person can make and act out your decision. Baalism may be beautiful, but ethically it is ridiculous, for it recognizes neither that I am a person nor that I am responsible to my Maker.

It is precisely for this reason that the Bible refuses to talk of God in any terms other than personal. The God of the Bible is never an *it* or a *one* or a *being*. He is portrayed as a *person*, with all of the emotions and will and intellect belonging to personality. Indeed, the Bible almost crudely describes the personhood of God, as if it

94

wished to embed its anthropomorphisms [7] and anthropopathisms [8] firmly within our consciousness. God, it says, has hands and fingers and arms (I Sam. 5:6; Ps. 8:3; Isa. 52:10). He hears with ears (Num. 11:1; II Kings 19:16) and meets man face to face (Gen. 32:30). He laughs and smells and whistles (Ps. 2:4; Gen. 8:21; Isa. 7:18). He hates and rejoices and regrets (Deut. 16:22; Isa. 61:8; 62:5; Gen. 6:6). He loves with a love exceeding understanding (Hos. 11:1-9), and he mourns terribly over the children he has lost (Jer. 31:20).

Moreover, these pictures of God's personality are not at all found only in the primitive strands of the Bible. It is precisely the prophets, with their high ethical religion, who use the most vivid anthropomorphisms. In Second Isaiah's soaring hymns of praise (Isa. 40–55), God is a mighty man of war, crying out and shouting aloud as he wades into the fray (Isa. 42:13). Or more shocking still, God is compared to a woman screaming and gasping in childbirth (Isa. 42:14). In the writings of the Yahwist, who is one of the most profound theologians of the Old Testament, God walks in the garden of Eden in the cool of the day (Gen. 3:8); he personally shuts the door of Noah's ark to make sure it is tightly sealed (Gen. 7:16); he comes down to inspect man's sinful work at Babel (Gen. 11:5) and at Sodom and Gomorrah (Gen. 18:21). But it is the New Testament which uses the most anthropomorphic language of all. For there God comes to earth in the full concreteness of human flesh, sharing completely in our life's feelings and thoughts and temptations. There is no thought in the New Testament that it is all just pictorial language. God becomes man in Jesus of Nazareth, in the ultimate anthropomorphism.

We sophisticated moderns may be just a little scandalized by the biblical mode of thought. To think that the Ultimate, the Absolute,

[7] The ascription to God of human form.
[8] The ascription to God of human emotions.

Being, the One, is "limited" by personality! But the Scriptures consistently maintain their view with a total lack of embarrassment, because only if God is viewed as personal are we required to answer to him. We may take an indifferent attitude toward an impersonal one or an unconscious life force. We may ignore an absolute or a vague divine ultimate. But we cannot ignore or be neutral toward a God who is personal. He confronts us in terms of love, of will, of anger, of grief, of demand. His very personhood demands the positive or negative response of our person.

Furthermore, the response we make to the person of God must involve our whole personality. An abstract one can be accepted or rejected only with the intellect. An impersonal being or mystical presence can be repugnant or pleasing only to the emotions. But when the God who has made us to serve him is person in all of his fullness, he demands from us the full response of our total personality. He requires from us the response of mind and will and emotion, the outpouring of our total selves in adoration and obedience and belief. We either love God with our heart and soul and mind together (Matt. 22:37), or we have rejected him by the attempt to limit his personal demand to one facet of our personalities.

It is for this reason that the intellectual acceptance of mere dogmas is not enough in the Christian faith. You may be among the respected few who can mouth all of the proper theological phrases within your own religious circle. You may even be well-read and sophisticated when it comes to theological understanding. But both Old and New Testaments pour contempt on phrases and learning alone:

> And the Lord said:
> "Because this people draw near with their mouth
>   and honor me with their lips,
>   while their hearts are far from me,

96

and their fear of me is a commandment of men learned
   by rote;
therefore, behold, I will again
   do marvelous things with this people,
   wonderful and marvelous; [i.e., in judgment]
and the wisdom of their wise men shall perish,
   and the discernment of their discerning men shall be hid"
                                          (Isa. 29:13-14).

And if I have prophetic powers, and understand all mysteries and all
knowledge, and if I have all faith, so as to remove mountains, but
have not love, I am nothing. . . . Love never ends; as for prophecy, it
will pass away; as for tongues, they will cease, as for knowledge, it
will pass away (I Cor. 13:2, 8).

God requires from us the obedience of our total selves, the dedication to his lordship of our minds and wills and hearts.

On the other hand, however, this is another reason why we
women too are required to serve God with our minds as well as
our emotions. We have been emotionally feeling our way along in
the church's life for decades in America. But the response required
of us by the personhood of God must be one of mind and understanding as well. It is all very well to say we are disinterested in
theology and intellectual matters. The fact is that God's requirement
demands that we also think.

Similarly, God's total demand upon our total personalities is also
the reason for his refusal to force us to do his will. I am often asked
by women in our churches, "Why doesn't God just *make* us do
what he wants?" But God will not be satisfied without our dedication of our wills to him, too. If he took over and coerced our
wills, they would never belong to him. He is a person, who wants
from us the full measure of our personhood, the answering "yes"

of our personality to his personality, as he is revealed in Jesus Christ.

Finally, it is only when God is known as personal that his goal is seen to be a community, for only a God of personhood desires to create and to dwell in a fellowship. A mystical life force can be felt and worshiped in complete detachment from the rest of mankind. An abstract absolute can be apprehended in the privacy of one's own intellect. But a personal God who measures obedience in terms of how we love or hate, is a God who demands that we have always something to do with our fellow men. Our response to him cannot be in abstract or mystical terms. It is acted out concretely in everything we think or do in the community in which he has placed us. When God is so personal that his one goal for his world is the creation of a new community, every relation of our lives takes on the form of an acceptance or a rejection of that goal. As we forgive the woman next door, we say "yes" or "no" to God's goal. As we react to those in our homes, we disrupt or affirm God's fellowship. The personal God of the Bible, unlike a god of nature, demands from us responsible and total reaction to his personhood within the framework of a community.

It seems clear, then, that the biblical faith does reject and necessarily must reject every form of baalism, every form of belief which would try to know God fully through the medium of his creation. That creation is not only inadequate to reveal the God of the Bible. Its very character, when seen apart from the Word, perverts our understanding and acceptance of the lordship of God. In the place of an eternal King, it can reveal only a transitory and powerless being, who is tied to the world as it is. For the purpose of the Lord of history, it substitutes a meaningless and unending cyclicism. In the stead of God's personal demand for responsible individualism in the context of community, it asks only the loss of self and identity through absorption into an impersonal one. Natural religion, apart from the Word, leads inevitably to error and idolatry. In the light of the biblical witness, it cannot be other than totally rejected.

The church in America, in this era, needs to ponder these facts. But most of all, we women need to understand and to act on them. We—perhaps more than any others—have been the idolaters in America, foolishly trying to find our God revealed in the natural world, ignorantly perpetuating the ancient's chant, "O Baal, answer us!" (I Kings 18:26). Baalism and life in Jesus Christ have nothing to do with one another. It is time we put away our idols and followed after the Master.

CHAPTER IV

WHEN YOU WALK THROUGH FIRE

There is a third way in which the theological understanding of American women has proved itself inadequate. Besides our failure to apprehend the true nature of our relationship to God (Ch. II), along with our idolatrous worship of Baal in the religion of nature (Ch. III), we women have often failed to understand the meaning and importance of the judgment of God.

In fact, it is commonplace among women's groups in modern America to reject completely the thought of God as Judge. This is a primitive concept, it is held, beyond which we have progressed. According to the view held by many women, man's religion in ancient days was one of fear before a God of wrath. Primitive man had to bring gifts and make sacrifices to appease the anger of his God. But now we know through Jesus Christ that God is a God of love, who desires our good and who loves us completely even when we are unlovable. To think therefore, many women hold, that God judges us or is wrathful is to contradict the revelation of himself which he has given in Jesus Christ.

This is one of the excuses women often give for their rejection or ignorance of the Old Testament. They think it witnesses only to a God of judgment, before whose anger primitive Old Testament man quaked in unreasoning fear. Such a view toward the Old Testament is, of course, a complete misunderstanding of the message of the entire Bible.

As we have noted before in our discussion (Ch. II), the God of the Bible is from the first a loving Lord, who creates man to live in community in the midst of a good and peaceful world. When man's sin introduces chaos and evil into his creation, the one goal of God becomes the restoration of a godly fellowship. To achieve his purpose, God becomes Father and Husband to a people, pouring out upon his adopted Israel a faithful and forgiving love. When despite his mercy Israel persists as a stubborn and rebellious son, God in the person of his begotten Son, takes on and fulfills Israel's role, accepting even the death of the cross that all may have life under his lordship. From beginning to end, through Old Testament and New, the message is one of incredible love. And the goal of love, which is reached in Christ, is announced already in Genesis (12:1-3). The Old Testament cannot be rejected on the grounds that the New outdates it, for its God is the Father of Jesus Christ and its words of promise are the very words which are made flesh in Jesus of Nazareth. Without the witness to God in the Old Testament, Jesus Christ and his church are incomprehensible.[1]

Thus, to live by trust in Jesus Christ—to be members of his new community—is to live by the revelation which is given of God

[1] For a complete discussion, see Paul and Elizabeth Achtemeier, *The Old Testament Roots of Our Faith* (Nashville: Abingdon Press, 1962).

through New Testament *and* Old. And there can be no doubt that in the Old Testament, God judges his people.

We are all familiar with the symbolic stories of the expulsion from the Garden of Eden (Gen. 3), of the sentence imposed on the murderer Cain to "be a fugitive and a wanderer on the earth" (Gen. 4:12), of the worldwide deluge let loose on man for his rebellion in the time of Noah (Gen. 6–9). These are themes which are ever repeated in drama and poetry and fable, and we accept them naturally as profound parts of mankind's mythico-religious heritage.

But we are less familiar with the stories of the judgments of God upon Israel herself. And these stories make up a large portion of the entire Old Testament history. There are Israel's forty years of penal wandering through the pits and dust of the desert, and the refusal to allow the aged Moses to cross into the land of promise. There is the constant clang of battle from an Israel punished with attack in the age of the Judges. There are the demented ragings of the rejected Saul and the mourning of the adulterous David over his sons. At the end there is the sound of Rachel crying for her children, the ten lost tribes of the North (cf. Jer. 31:15), and there is the sight of exiled Judah weeping by the waters of Babylon (Ps. 137). Throughout its pages the Old Testament sounds forth an agonized antiphony to God's love—the wail of a dismayed and plundered Israel, suffering because she has mistrusted that love. The Lord responds to his people's sin. He responds with terrible judgments. And because he loves his son Israel so much, it seems that his judgments are all the more fierce. As he tells his people through the words of his prophet Amos:

> You only have I known
> of all the families of the earth;

> therefore I will punish you
> for all your iniquities (Amos 3:2).

God's chosen people are marked out for judgment, it seems, precisely because they are chosen. Their special place in the plan of God makes it necessary that they be afflicted.

Yet God's judgments in the proclamation of the Old Testament are not limited to Israel. Certainly they fall first and most heavily upon the elected of God—a thought which the church must bear in mind in every age and situation. But the prophets include the punishment of Israel in the framework of a wider reckoning, in which the Lord of history calls every nation to account for its rebellion against him. We see this quite plainly in Joel 3, with its "multitudes, multitudes, in the valley of decision!" (Joel 3:14), or in the court scenes from Second Isaiah, where the people are summoned to bring forth their witnesses to justify them before the Lord (Isa. 41:1, 21; 43:9; 44:6-7; 45:20-21). But nowhere is God's worldwide judgment made more clear than in the words of Jeremiah (Ch. 25). The prophet portrays all nations forced to drink from God's cup of wrath and staggering:

Then you shall say to them, "Thus says the Lord of hosts, the God of Israel: Drink, be drunk and vomit, fall and rise no more, because of the sword which I am sending among you."

And if they refuse to accept the cup from your hand to drink, then you shall say to them, "Thus says the Lord of hosts: You must drink! For behold, I begin to work evil at the city which is called by my name [i.e., Jerusalem], and shall you go unpunished? You shall not go unpunished, for I am summoning a sword against all the inhabitants of the earth, says the Lord of hosts."

You, therefore, shall prophesy against them all these words, and say to them:

"The Lord will roar from on high,
    and from his holy habitation utter his voice;
he will roar mightily against his fold,
    and shout, like those who tread grapes,
    against all the inhabitants of the earth.
The clamor will resound to the ends of the earth,
    for the Lord has an indictment against the nations;
he is entering into judgment with all flesh,
    and the wicked he will put to the sword,
                    says the Lord" (Jer. 25:27-31).

Despite the distaste which such passages arouse in us toward the Old Testament, it is necessary that we confront their message realistically and fully. For the fact is that they are completely consonant with the proclamation of the New Testament, and in Jesus Christ their words, too, are fulfilled.

Certainly Jesus spoke many words of judgment against his contemporaries during his ministry. We have only to read a passage like Matthew 23 to become aware of the depth of his vehemence against the religious leaders of his time. His words belie the usual saccharine portrayal of him as a sweet and gentle spiritualist. Similarly, when he speaks of the final judgment of God upon all of us (Matt. 25; Mark 8:34-38; 9:42-50; Luke 13:22-30; 20:9-18, etc.), he sets the issue in the sternest terms of our decisions for or against him, and the talk is of curse or blessing, eternal punishment or life.

But it is not merely Jesus' teachings which pose the judgment of God. It is his person, his presence among us, which places us before God the Judge. "What do you think of the Christ?" (Matt. 22:42). That is the question which we are forced to confront in Jesus of Nazareth. The way we answer it determines whether or not we are willing to place our lives in the hands of God the Lord. Is the man Christ Jesus the only way to God the Father? Is God at work in his person to set up his kingdom on earth? Is this carpenter from

104

Nazareth the one source of our hope and comfort in life and after death? Because of Christ we have to answer these questions before the bar of the ultimate Judge, not only theoretically and dogmatically, but practically, every day of our lives.

Our answers in the tribunal, however, are very plainly negative. We don't place our trust in Jesus Christ. We crucify him. Try as we may to escape that tale of Golgotha and its horrors, we have to admit that we were there and that it is the story of our lives. Like those Romans and Jews at the foot of the cross, we do the Son of God to death. And we work the deed with some of the finest virtue we can muster. We summon the structure of our law to execute the innocent. We call upon our religious sensibilities to cast out the supposed sinner. We cite the necessity of order and business to trample the weak and needful. And every time we do so to one of the least of our brethren, we do it to Christ. We circle our power structures around the living body of God's love, and then we move in on him with our nails, hammering away in our righteousness until love incarnate is done to death. We can't stand that mercy-made-flesh in actual deed. We have to keep hanging him on the gallows of our "goodness."

As a result, the cross of Christ is not only the seal of God's forgiveness. It is at the same time the ineradicable symbol of God's wrath against us. In the words of the Fourth Gospel: "This is the judgment, that the light has come into the world, and men loved darkness rather than light, because their deeds were evil" (John 3:19). This is the unassailable proof of our guilt before the bar of God—that our very law and piety and claims to goodness lead us to destroy God's Son. In the person of Christ, God pronounces that sentence of guilt which he promised in the words of his prophets, and all mankind is seen to be worthy of death in the light of Jesus Christ. With the death of Christ, all of our claims to goodness and, therefore, to immortality die too. We are judged by God in Jesus of Nazareth and given over with him to the executioner.

1.

If we ignore these aspects of the total biblical faith, if we turn aside from the thought of God's judgment, if we attempt to skip over Lent's penitential somberness in our preference for a happy Easter, we will not only pervert our Christian faith; we may lose it altogether. Indeed, the evidence from the lives of many American women points to the fact of their lostness, as they attempt to find a realm in which God no longer is Judge.

There is that large pathetic group, whom we mentioned before (Ch. I): women who are searching for their own inner peace. Because they ignore the fact that in Christ they are condemned as well as forgiven, they think they can come to permanent terms with God on the basis of their *status quo*. They seize only on Christ's promise that he gives to them his peace (John 14:27), turning aside from the fact that he also promises them a sword (Matt. 10:34). They cling to the fact that Christ has overcome the world, but they close their ears to the same word in which he says they shall nevertheless have tribulation (John 16:33). They desire to participate in the fullness of Christ's joy without the necessity of sharing his cup of sorrow (Mark 10:35-45). They want, in short, a life supported by the victory of the resurrection, without the necessity of bearing a cross and undergoing a crucifixion (Mark 8:34).

Much less definable among the wanderers from the judgment of God is a large group of women within the solid core of the church. These women share many of the characteristics of the most dedicated. They have a real faith which undergirds their lives. Frequently, they suffer for their beliefs in silent patience and hope. Often they sustain our corporate life with their prayers and their activities. But one fact separates them from the community of their fellow Christians. They do not know that despite all their faithfulness, they are still "unworthy servants" before God (Luke 17:7-10). It never occurs to them to doubt the vitality and validity of their faith. They bear with all of life's struggles and sufferings in the certainty that their reward will be great in the kingdom. They never know that terrible moment of despair in which the crown of life seems unattainable. In fact, they would never say with Paul, "Not that I have already obtained this or am already perfect" (Phil. 3:12). In some sense, in their own minds, they are already perfect, because their faith is unshakable and their dedication unquestioned. They look forward only to the confirmation of their certainties.

In short, these women are the modern Pharisees among us, and like their counterparts in the days of Jesus, they are not intentionally unfaithful to God nor unmistakably evil. But they bear about them an awful pride which makes them sometimes more destructive than the godless, because they are able to act toward their fellow men in such certainty of their position. There is missing from their deportment toward others primarily the quality of compassion—compassion which is born of the knowledge that we need terribly God's compassion ourselves.

When we confront God's judgment in Jesus Christ, there can be only one reaction, the prayer of the publican portrayed for us in the parable of Jesus: "God, be merciful to me a sinner!" (Luke 18:13.) Our whole existence is placed under doubt by the cross of Christ—everything we are, all the things we do, every belief we hold. And the only hope of living left open to us is to throw ourselves on the mercy of the court: "God, be merciful to me a sinner!" It is in that act of confession alone that we have hope of justification, for it is in that act alone that we appeal to God's forgiveness in Christ. The woman who does not know she is condemned, however, can never realize that she is the recipient of mercy (Matt. 9:10-13). The real joy, the real certainty, and the real compassion of the Christian faith will always escape her. She will never know how to forgive her fellows, because she will never really realize, that when she stood naked and defenseless before God the Judge, he forgave her in Jesus Christ (cf. Matt. 18:23-35; Luke 6:27-42).

The Pharisees among us, by reason of their pride, can work some awful deeds of destruction. But perhaps no group which seeks to ignore the judgment of God is more vagrant or more destructive than those whom we might call "in-group Christians." These are the women among us who absolutize their own community. They see in their own family or their own church or their own group or their own nation the realization of the kingdom of God. As a result, they seek to impose the will and the structure of their particular society upon the world around them. In the process, they label opponents and dissenters as unchristian or subversive.

We find such females among the widest variety of groups. They are those women in every neighborhood who believe that in their family alone children are being raised properly. They are the members of the zealous sects which lay sole claim to God's truth. They are the participants in the civic groups which have the one pattern for the community's life. They are the vocal political factions who see in their party or candidate's views the expression of the will of God. Everywhere they march with determination: to scold the neighbor's children playing on the front lawn; to censor the books in the local schools and to put "the fear of God" into librarians; to condemn the mayor or perhaps the pastor for his "rightist" or "leftist" tendencies; to expose a national organization as deviationist or unpatriotic; to insist on an American-style democracy in Africa or in Asia. They are a kind of Pharisee, by the popular definition of the term, but Pharisees who think that the kingdom has already come. In their group, they believe, the true community of God has been realized. Their mission in life therefore becomes to impose that community on everyone else. Their "in-group" life is never subject to the judgment of God. It is only those outside their body who stand in need of correction and salvation.

Fortunately for us women who think to escape our God the Judge (and what one among us is not guilty of such a tactic?) the Lord of our lives does not let us flee, free from his condemnation. He is always shaking and sifting us in his great sieve of providence, and we know our lives to be winnowed and altered despite our efforts to prevent it. We find a "peace," and then tragedy strikes at someone dear to our hearts. Or anxieties or awareness of the world's awful need creep in to upset our serenity. We establish a reputation for righteousness and begin to take our salvation for granted, but our efforts toward community fall apart, and we are frustrated by our failure to love. We establish a group in which life seems to be good, but we have to contend with the misunderstanding and hostility of the world toward our motives, and we become perplexed because others do not view the situation from our perspective. We set up the kingdom of God on earth, we believe, only to find it threatened within and without. Time passes, our kingdom totters, and passes away as does all else. There is a cross raised over our lives, a cross of continual judgment, and all we do and hope and believe is placed under the shadow of its sentence. Looking at that cross, we well may use the words of the psalmist to address the figure upon it:

> Thou turnest man back to the dust,
>   and sayest, "Turn back, O children of men!"
> For a thousand years in thy sight,
>   are but as yesterday when it is past,
>   or as a watch in the night.

Thou dost sweep men away; they are like a dream,
  like grass which is removed in the morning:
in the morning it flourishes and is renewed;
  in the evening it fades and withers.

For we are consumed by thy anger;
  by thy wrath we are overwhelmed.
Thou hast set our iniquities before thee,
  our secret sins in the light of thy countenance.

For all our days pass away under thy wrath,
  our years come to an end like a sigh.
The years of our life are threescore and ten,
  or even by reason of strength fourscore;
yet their span is but toil and trouble;
  they are soon gone, and we fly away.

Who considers the power of thy anger,
  and thy wrath according to the fear of thee?
So teach us to number our days
  that we may get a heart of wisdom (Ps. 90:3-12).

There is no realm in the world of mankind where we can escape God the Judge. We simply have to "get a heart of wisdom" and come to terms with our condemnation. Some of our modern authors and playwrights and artists have been pointing to this fact for some time. But others of them have slipped into fatalism or cynicism or despair, because they do not know *why* God acts in judgment. We shall make exactly the same mistakes unless we understand the reasons for the wrath of God.

2.

It seems doubtful that there is any passage in the Bible in which God's judgment is simply punitive. God does, to be sure, sometimes

110

level terrible destructions against sinful mankind. And his work has all of the appearance of a rage let loose against rebellion. In the book of Ezekiel, we read over and over that he will be satisfied in his wrath only when Israel has been completely and mercilessly destroyed. Rebellion against God on the part of man is a challenge to God's power to rule, and his answering judgment is often swift and unequivocal in its proof of his lordship. And yet, the God of Old and New Israel does not punish for the sake of punishing, and the popular conception of the wrath of God as the emotion of a proud Avenger actually has no support in the witness of the biblical text.

One evidence of this is the fact that God suffers so much when he judges. It is characteristic of the prophets of Israel that their words manifest God's emotions,[2] and for all of their stern acceptance of the death of Israel, they weep unceasingly over her downfall:

> My grief is beyond healing,
>   my heart is sick within me.
> Hark, the cry of the daughter of my people
>   from the length and breadth of the land:
> "Is the Lord not in Zion?
>   Is her King not in her?"
> "Why have they provoked me to anger with their graven
>   images,
>   and with their foreign idols?"
> "The harvest is past, the summer is ended,
>   and we are not saved."
> For the wound of the daughter of my people is my heart
>   wounded,
>   I mourn, and dismay has taken hold on me.

[2] For a complete discussion, see Abraham Heschel, *The Prophets* (New York: Harper & Row, 1962).

111

> Is there no balm in Gilead?
>   Is there no physician there?
> Why then has the health of the daughter of my people
>   not been restored?
> O that my head were waters,
>   and my eyes a fountain of tears,
> that I might weep day and night
>   for the slain of the daughter of my people! (Jer. 8:18-9:1.)

Not only Jeremiah mourns Israel's death in these words. They mirror, too, the mourning of God who regrets, as only he can regret, that Israel has been unfaithful (cf. Hos. 11:1-11). In fact, even Ezekiel, who is the coldest and sternest among the prophets, pronounces that God takes no pleasure in the death of the wicked:

Cast away from you all the transgressions which you have committed against me, and get yourselves a new heart and a new spirit! Why will you die, O house of Israel? For I have no pleasure in the death of anyone, says the Lord God; so turn, and live.

> (Ezek. 18:31-32; cf. 33:11.)

God does not delight in his actions as Judge. Rather, it costs him something to bring destruction upon his people. In the Old Testament, it costs him terrible grief. In the New Testament, it costs him finally his only begotten Son.

Furthermore, God's actions in judgment are never seen in the Bible as final. The ruin God brings upon Israel is not the ultimate goal he seeks. Thus, the prophet Isaiah can call God's deeds of wrath "strange" and term his works of condemnation "alien" to his proper work (Isa. 28:21). God does not punish men simply for the sake of punishing. There lies a reason behind his judgments, a purpose which rules out all thought of vengeance.

Because of this fact, no tragedy or disaster in our lives should ever be viewed only as God's punishment. God is not just expressing his anger with us for some sin we have committed. It is contrary to the biblical faith ever to view a misfortune simply as a punishment, whether that misfortune has befallen us or one of our acquaintances. God seeks a goal beyond punishment when he intervenes in our world in judgment. There is a purpose to what God does and to what therefore happens in our lives.

Perhaps nowhere is this more clearly expressed than in Deut. 4:24, where it is stated that the Lord our God is a "devouring fire" and "a jealous God." Here God's "fire," a simile for his judgment (cf. Pss. 68:2; 78:21; Isa. 30:27; Jer. 15:14; Mic. 1:4; Mal. 3:2), is expressly connected with his jealousy. The reason he judges is because he is a jealous God (cf. Exod. 20:5; 34:14; Ezek. 5:13; I Cor. 10:22).

The jealousy of God is not to be understood, however, according to our popular definitions. It has nothing to do with the self-seeking insecurity characteristic of human jealousy. It does not signify that God is some sort of ugly, green-eyed monster. Rather, the word for "jealousy" in the Hebrew is the same word as is used for "zeal" (*qannā'*), and to say that the God of the Bible is jealous is to say that he is zealous. God is full of zeal. He has an ardent and active interest in us. He wants to see that we become something and that we accomplish something. He wants to see, in short, that we achieve a goal. God judges, God is jealous, because he has a goal and a purpose for our lives (cf. Zech. 8:1-3). And all his acts of destruction and judgment are directed toward reaching that goal. The goal is, as we have seen previously (Ch. II), the establishment of a new community under his lordship. God's judgments are one means he uses to extend his kingship over the earth.

As a result, throughout the Bible, God's judgments may take different forms, but everywhere they are seen from the perspective of God's ultimate goal of community. Sometimes God acts destructively to educate his people. For example, Amos 4:6-11 tells us that God sent famine, drought, crop failures, illnesses, and military defeats upon Israel, all in an attempt to teach his people that they were dependent upon him (cf. Hos. 2:2-7). He wanted to show Israel that her life as a people lay in faithful obedience to his will. He thus tried to educate her by showing her the destructive results of rebellion and unfaithfulness (cf. Ps. 78). God hoped that as Israel learned the insufficiency of her own power to save herself, she would be led to look only to him for strength and salvation.

It is for this reason that the psalmist can say, "Blessed is the man whom thou dost chasten, O Lord" (Ps. 94:12a). He who is subjected to the judgment of God has the opportunity to learn he is in error (cf. Jer. 2:19). Far from being a sign of God's rejection and abandonment, suffering is in this view an evidence of God's love and concern (cf. II Sam. 7:14-15; Jer. 30:11). God afflicts in order to teach us the way to live under his kingship (Heb. 12:5-11; cf. Rom. 5:3). As his Word puts it in the Apocalypse of John: "Those whom I love, I reprove and chasten; so be zealous and repent" (Rev. 3:19).

By the same token God's judgments upon Israel are often viewed as purifying. God subjects his people to the fire of his wrath in order to refine out their dross (Isa. 1:25; 48:10; Zech. 13:9; Mal. 3:3; cf. Jer. 6:29; Ezek. 22:17-22; 24:1-14). Or he allows his people to undergo suffering in order to cleanse them of their evil (Ezek. 20:33-38; Dan. 11:35). Sometimes, only in this way, can God fit his people for life in the kingdom or make them effective instruments of his redemptive working in the world.

There is no sentimental compromise in the Bible by which the new life can be superimposed on the old. The new cloth cannot be used merely to patch up the old garment, and the new wine cannot be poured into the old weak wineskins (Luke 5:36-39). Rather, to have newness of life, the old life with its ways must be destroyed.

The seed must fall in the ground and die (John 12:24; cf. I Cor. 15:36), the old birth give place to a new (John 3:3), the rebellious spirit and the heart of stone be replaced with obedient ones (Ezek. 11:19; 36:26-27). In short our old evil selves must be crucified in order that we may be raised to new life. And it is sometimes with the flame of his judgments and afflictions that God accomplishes the job. Prideful ways are suddenly humbled by sickness or emotional ruin; a family slowly falls apart or a business meets with disaster; a way of life is forcibly outdated by social protest and violence; a nation's plans and calculations are upset by a leader's sudden death. Overnight the pattern and supports of our life are removed and gone (cf. Isa. 3:1-5), and we are faced with the necessity of a totally new manner of existence. To the Bible's way of thinking, the individual and corporate deaths we undergo cannot be separated from the purpose of God. Often God uses them to give us the possibility of resurrection into new life. It is by the destruction of Israel that God gives her the hope of becoming a new people. And it is by the crucifixion of his Son that God inaugurates his kingdom on earth. Throughout the Bible, death is the necessary presupposition of new life under God's lordship. It is with his refining and destroying furnace of judgment that God often kills in order to make alive.

There is a third view of the judgments of God manifested in the Bible. With his afflictions God educates and purifies, but he also uses suffering redemptively. At times, Israel is called to sacrifice herself for the sake of the rest of the world. This is especially clear in the prophecies of Second Isaiah. Israel is called to receive *double* punishment for all her sins (Isa. 40:2), not because God is unjust, but because he is loving. He wishes to use Israel's faith from the midst of innocent suffering as a witness to all the world, in order that all nations will be drawn into the congregation of the people of God (Isa. 52:13-53:12). Israel's witness to the activity of God, despite her

115

desperate situation, will make clear to all the nations the presence of the Lord in their lives. Israel is asked to sacrifice herself for the redemption of all. As we have pointed out in Chapter II, it is this role of the Suffering Servant which is finally taken up and fulfilled by Christ on the cross.

This view of suffering as a vicarious sacrifice for the benefit of others is, however, manifested throughout the total Bible. Abraham leaves everything behind to begin the journey to the land of promise (Gen. 12:1), just as later the apostle Paul suffers all things as loss for the sake of gaining Christ (Phil. 3:7-8). And when we look at the lives of the prophets, we find them bearing a crushing weight of agony for the sake of the Word. Elijah is forced to flee for his life. Amos is driven from the capital. Hosea is asked to live with a prostitute. Ezekiel's wife is taken by death. Isaiah is mocked by king and drunkards. Jeremiah's whole life is suffering: he is driven out of the town of his birth and denounced by his family and friends; he is charged with madness, placed first in the stocks, and then in an abondoned cistern; he is called a traitor to his country and a prophet of lies; finally he is forcibly taken to Egypt where he remains until his death. There is no evidence in any of their writings that the prophets believed God called them to make them happy. Their personal welfare seems of total indifference to the Lord who commands their lives. Rather, God uses the prophets to further his will on the earth, and the prophets, too, suffer the loss of all things for the sake of that will.

It is not surprising, therefore, that God can ask his Son to die for his kingdom. Throughout the Bible, God has used men's sacrifice as the means of fulfilling his purpose. In the beginning the hapless troops of Egypt gave their lives to glorify God at the Sea of Reeds (or the "Red Sea," Exod. 14-15), just as in the Gospel of John a man was born blind in order that Jesus might one day be glorified in Jerusalem (John 9). Running throughout the Bible is the conviction that nothing is so precious as God's kingdom (Matt. 13:45-46), and men are required—sometimes even without their knowledge—to give up goods, kindred, happiness, health, even life itself, in order that the kingdom may come. Finally, God's Son is subjected to reviling and torturous death, in order that God may at last begin his new community on earth.

We find evidences in our lives, too, that God requires us to suffer for his purpose. Many mates are asked to bear silently and charitably with the dissatisfactions of unhappy marriages, in order that their children not be torn or destroyed by divorce's necessity of choosing between parents. Many neighbors are called to forgive constantly in order to preserve a community. Many knowing pain or loneliness are required to forget themselves, in order that their joy in Christ may be made manifest to their world. God always asks that we give ourselves for the sake of a higher good. But the Bible's point is that there really is no good outside the realm of God's rule. From the Bible's perspective nothing and no one can give life to man except the Lord of life. And thus, the Bible sees the total human enterprise as expendable for the abundant life of God's kingdom. God may afflict in his judgments; he may ask of us total sacrifice. But the purpose behind every one of his acts is the loving redemption of his world.

It is true that we are judged and given over to death by the cross of Christ. But it is also true that that cross is not the end of the story. God raises his Son from the grave into a new and eternal life. And just as we die in Christ, we are also made alive in him. Though God judges us in Jesus Christ—judges us throughout our lives, by suffering, affliction, catastrophe, evil—he overcomes his wrath with his love. Indeed, his judgments are made an instrument of his forgiveness and his mercy, and he uses them to lead us and our world into the life of his new community. By his cross God makes possible the resurrection. By his wrath God educates and purifies and redeems. By the means of his judgment he works in love to establish his kingdom over all the earth.

3.

The remarkable characteristic of the biblical faith is the persistence with which it holds these views. And perhaps it is this one characteristic, more than any other, which distinguishes and sets apart the person of biblical faith: the ability to perceive God working toward his kingdom in the midst of every event, the faith that God is actively present and shaping history according to his purpose.

For example, when we read the biblical accounts of the siege and destruction of Jerusalem, we are almost overwhelmed by the horrors of the situation. The city's life is reduced to chaos and cannabalism by the lack of food and water during the siege:

> The tongue of the nursling cleaves
> to the roof of its mouth for thirst;
> the children beg for food,
> but no one gives to them.

> Those who feasted on dainties
> perish in the streets;
> those who were brought up in purple
> lie on ash heaps.

> For the chastisement of the daughter of my people has
> been greater
> than the punishment of Sodom,
> which was overthrown in a moment,
> no hand being laid on it.

Her princes were purer than snow,
  whiter than milk;
their bodies were more ruddy than coral,
  the beauty of their form was like sapphire.

Now their visage is blacker than soot,
  they are not recognized in the streets;
their skin has shriveled upon their bones,
  it has become as dry as wood.

Happier were the victims of the sword
  than the victims of hunger,
who pined away, stricken
  by want of the fruits of the field.

The hands of compassionate women
  have boiled their own children;
they became their food
  in the destruction of the daughter of my people
    (Lam. 4:4-10; cf. Ezek. 4:16-17; 5:10).

Even in the midst of these horrors, however, the biblical writers refuse to believe that God is not actively present. In fact, so sure are they that God is in control of their lives, that they ascribe the suffering they are undergoing to the hand of God himself:

Who has commanded and it came to pass,
  unless the Lord has ordained it?
Is it not from the mouth of the Most High
  that good and evil come? (Lam. 3:37-38; cf. Isa. 45:7.)

To the Bible's way of thinking, nothing—not even the most gruesome suffering—can lie outside the purpose of God, not because God is evil, but because he is the Lord of history. All life, no matter what its situation, lies in the hands of God. From him it takes its ultimate source and from him it has its meaning.

This does not mean that the Bible ever considers suffering to be good in itself. The person of biblical faith never develops a "martyr complex," nor does he seek for ways to undergo punishment and affliction. The Bible's laments make it very clear that suffering is understood for what it is: a source of pain which is to be corrected or avoided, if possible in God's sight. Thus Jesus prays in Gethsemane, "My father, if it be possible, let this cup pass from me" (Matt. 26:39). But the Bible's point is that suffering and affliction are never meaningless, because they are encompassed in the larger framework of the purpose of God. God works through every event, even the most evil ones, to accomplish his ultimate purpose of redeeming human life. The prophet can therefore say,

> Who gave up Jacob to the spoiler,
>   and Israel to the robbers?
> Was it not the Lord, against whom we have sinned,
>   in whose ways they would not walk,
>   and whose law they would not obey? (Isa. 42:24.)

And when contemplating the cross of Christ, the New Testament can borrow only one affirmation:

> It was the will of the Lord to bruise him;
>   he has put him to grief (Isa. 53:10*ab*).

The purpose of God becomes the meaning and reason behind all historical events.

The biblical writers know, however, that God's purpose is a purpose of love, and thus their acceptance of the afflictions and judgments of God becomes a great hymn of witness to that love:

120

We are afflicted in every way, but not crushed; perplexed, but not driven to despair; persecuted, but not forsaken; struck down, but not destroyed; always carrying in the body the death of Jesus, so that the life of Jesus may also be manifested in our bodies (II Cor. 4:8-10).

Persecuted, imprisoned, ill, afflicted, the men of biblical faith are nevertheless buoyed along by the knowledge that God wills and is at work in their lives to do his good pleasure (Phil. 2:13). God works in all events to accomplish his purpose of love. It is in this faith that the judgments of God have their meaning.

Unless, through study and knowledge of the Bible, we come to share this faith, we shall never satisfactorily be able to come to terms with the judgments of God. We shall ever be searching for some mythical world where there is only "peace." We shall always be attempting to maintain our religious security and self-righteousness. We shall always be claiming for our group and its views an absolute position. But the biblical history, with its cross of Christ, will always contradict us, and unless we come to understand that history, we may eventually live out our days in bitterness or resignation or despair.

The woman who feels that her own ways are perfect will never grow in the life of faith, and if her life is suddenly subjected to trial, she can only feel that God has brought unjust and undeserved punishment upon her. "How can God do such a thing?" will be her perplexed or bitter cry. She will never be able to realize that God is working in her life in love, using even her suffering to fit her for life in his kingdom. We have to be willing to give up our own self-claims to perfection. We have to accept God the Judge. Otherwise the afflictions that come upon us will seem without purpose and meaning.

In the same manner we have to be willing to sacrifice our personal serenity. We have to accept the fact that God sometimes up-

sets us in order to accomplish his purpose. We are often asked to
bear the greatest emotional trials in order that God can work
through us in the life of a child or a friend or a relative. We are
always asked to be disturbed by injustice and need. We are always required to recognize that the world is not as God intended it and that
therefore it stands under God's constant refining judgment. God
will not let us cry, "Peace, peace," when there is no peace. He will
not let us resign ourselves to the evil *status quo*. God is Judge, who
will always prod and disturb and use us, until he brings his kingdom on earth, with its true and eternal peace.

Thus, we finally have to be willing to see every achievement and
group in our world as provisional, in order that all may ultimately
give way to the coming of the kingdom of God. We Christians share
the loves of this world with our fellow human beings. We love our
families, we dedicate ourselves to our communities, we have a
fierce patriotism for our nation. And family devotion and civic
pride and enlightened nationalism are necessary. (As I write this
book during a year abroad, I long for the life of the United States.
Surely there is no nation on earth with America's sense of freedom!)
But no family group and no community and no nation is the kingdom of God, and we dare not ever claim for them an absolute
position. We dare not try to impose their form as final on the rest
of humanity. All stand under the judgment of God. All must be
refined and perfected. All must be replaced by God's completed
community of love. Thus, despite our loves of earth, we must be
always "strangers and pilgrims" upon it, journeying toward God's
new realm of fulfillment and goodness and faith. If we want that
realm to come, we have to be willing to be judged. We have to be
willing to see ourselves as something less than perfect. We have to
be willing to be disciplined and destroyed and made alive, until
finally we conform to the goal which God has set for our lives. God
moves in certain sovereignty through history toward the goal of his

new community. If we want to participate in that community's new life, we too must be willing to count all things as loss for the sake of gaining its prize.

Our comfort, however, in the midst of affliction is that God is present with us, actively, tirelessly, lovingly working to fulfill his purpose for our lives. Through the words of Second Isaiah, he tells us:

> Fear not, for I have redeemed you;
>   I have called you by name, you are mine.
> When you pass through the water I will be with you,
>   and through the rivers, they shall not overwhelm you;
> when you walk through fire you shall not be burned,
>   and the flame shall not consume you.
> For I am the Lord your God,
>   the Holy One of Israel, your Savior (Isa. 43:1c-3b).

God does not say we do not have to walk through the fire. He promises only that he will be with us (cf. Exod. 3:12), and that he will work his redemption and accomplish his purpose of love (cf. Dan. 3).

God's presence with us in the midst of his judgments will not always be apparent. The faith of the biblical man or woman is not dependent on what he or she can see or feel (cf. John 20:29). We are not always granted the gift of a "religious experience" of God. There are days and months, and even years, when no personal "presence" is felt. Indeed, a "mystical experience" of God's reality is sometimes never known by the Christian, and such an experience should not be viewed as a necessity in the Christian's life. Further, there are times when prayer seems futile, so that we must cry out with the author of Lamentations,

> thou hast wrapped thyself with a cloud
>   so that no prayer can pass through (Lam. 3:44).

123

There are times when events seem devoid of God and when, as in the thought of some modern authors, nothing answers us back from the heavens but an empty and awful silence. But this is the essential nature of the biblical faith—that it believes God nevertheless present and that it believes him working in love despite all appearances to the contrary (cf. Luke 21:28). Faith, for the biblical man or woman, is clinging to the Word of God. It is trusting that God will fulfill that Word, according to his promise (cf. Heb. 11). It is "the assurance of things hoped for, the conviction of things not seen" (Heb. 11:1). Faith is flinging out God's "nevertheless!" against all the evidence. It is staking one's life on the fact that God is present and working in love to bring in his eternal kingdom.

In the light of the biblical story, with its culmination in the cross and resurrection, there can be no doubt that God will fulfill his Word and accomplish his loving purpose for our world. God began his kingdom in Jesus Christ. He will complete it in him. As we walk through fire, he is only actively leading us toward the perfection of that new community.

CHAPTER V

THE NEW COMMUNITY

The world of nature and the world of man are being moved toward the kingdom of God, propelled by the mighty and merciful hand of the God who has created them both.[1] From that fact every event of life takes its meaning and its purpose. In accordance with that fact we "saints in Christ" are called to shape our lives. The life of the new people of God is a life of trust, trust in the kingly rule of God made manifest in Jesus Christ.

Between these general theological statements and the life of the average housewife, however, there sometimes lies a vast realm of

---

[1] The reader must not confuse God's actions toward the goal of his kingdom with an evolutionary or progressive development of history and of nature. As we have seen, nature apart from God goes around in a circle, and human history can go down as well as up. God's kingdom develops out of neither, but is consistently pictured by the Bible as a radical and surprising in-breaking of a totally new reality into our finite realm. Cf. Matt. 24:36-44; Rev. 21:1.

misunderstanding and misapplication. We American women would like to apply the Word of God to our daily lives. But the truth is that we sometimes do not know how to do so. We do not know what the kingship of God has to do with the life of our households. We do not know how to trust in God's rule while being average American housewives.

The result is that many of us limit the life of trust only to the sphere of our local church. Its buildings and its activities set the border limits to the new community. Within the church's walls God may be acclaimed as King, but we seldom act as if God's rule actually extends beyond the sanctuary door. Outside the church is the realm of the practical, the sensible, the influential, and the actions of God are seldom applied to the events of our work-a-day existence. Perhaps the most common expression of this attitude is the often used phrase "stick to religion." Life is divided into sacred and secular, into God's realm and man's. God rules as Lord of the church for us, but not as the Lord of the world.

Many churches themselves have unwittingly fostered these positions, implying in the message they bring that the new community is limited to their confines. Thus, for example, their call is always to participate in *their* fellowships and programs. Their plea for money is framed in terms of giving contributions to the church itself. Their definition of "full-time Christian service" is limited to work within their structure. The implication is that only within their bounds can God be worshiped as the Lord. Time and money and service on "the outside" really do not count. The life of faith is properly lived within the organization of the church.

Such churches, then, become competitors in our world. They compete for their members' time and money and loyalty against all of the other "secular" demands made on their members' resources. They give the impression that it is disloyal to Christ to refuse to join the women's guild, and that somehow a woman really is not following the Master if she chooses to serve on a "secular" rather than a "sacred" (church) committee. As a friend of mine put it, "I feel guilty for spending so much time with the Scouts instead of with the church." God, for her, could only be served in his sacred ecclesiastical sphere.

It is precisely such an attitude, however, against which many of the prophets fought—the attempt to limit the sphere of God's rule and, therefore, the area of his new community. From the time of King David onward Israel's life became increasingly "secularized," with the monarchy attempting to replace the authority of the cult as the guide of the people's lives. Commerce, politics, law, the military—all were separated more or less from the traditional Mosaic religion, in the attempt to carve out a sphere of power free of the rule of God. As is the case in the churches mentioned above, the clergy sometimes supported such efforts, limiting the role of religion to worship and support of the state. Thus we find the prophet Amos being rebuked by a royal priest for meddling in politics in the capital city instead of sticking to religion (Amos 7:12-13). Elijah earlier is called the "troubler of Israel" (I Kings 18:17) for criticizing King Ahab, and he finally engages in a life-and-death dispute with Ahab's notorious queen Jezebel (I Kings 19; 21). But the prophets, with their Word of God, would not bow to the criticisms of them. "I have not troubled Israel," replied Elijah to Ahab, "but you have, and your father's house, because you have forsaken the commandments of the Lord" (I Kings 18:18). The prophets would not limit the sovereignty of their God. They knew his rule extended into royal palace and over peasant's field. They saw that it gave the standard for the marketplace and even for the conduct of war. They held it out as the basis for family life and for the relations between neighbors. God's kingship, in the faith of the prophets, was the basic fact of all existence. To the fact of God's rule the whole of life was to be shaped and conformed.

If the Christian Church professes to live by the Word of God, surely its practice and proclamation can be no different than that of the prophets. The life and death and resurrection of Jesus Christ did not reveal a limited Lord. They made certain to men the sovereignty of God over the whole of existence. They proclaimed God's power to legislate over all life and death. They revealed the good news that God governs his world both now and for all time to come.

Therefore, God is to be served as the Lord not only within a church. His rule is to be acknowledged and trusted in every realm of life. And his rule is to be seen as the decisive factor in the immediate now. It is true that God's kingdom, with its perfection, still lies in the future. It is true that the natural world and the history of men have not been brought to their final goal by God. Nevertheless, in Jesus Christ, God began his new community, and by trust in God through Jesus Christ we begin our participation in its life. As Paul put it, "Now we see in a mirror dimly, but then face to face" (I Cor. 13:12). The perfection of our lives and of our world lies in the kingdom to come. But the trust in God's lordship that *will* be required of us is the trust required of us *now*. And we begin our new life under God by rendering him immediate allegiance.

Indeed, this is what the church of Jesus Christ is: the company of those who trust God's lordship, as that lordship has been revealed in God's Word and made flesh in Jesus Christ. The church is not confined to the activities of a group in a particular building. It is not a community with a program set over against all other activities. It is not an organization with leaders and a budget dedicated to preserving an ecclesiastical machinery. The church is the fellowship of all those who trust in God the King. And because the King reigns over all life, the church's trusting fellowship may also be found everywhere. In families, among neighbors, in places of business, between friends, wherever we live in trust—there the church of Jesus Christ actually exists and acts. There is found the new and faithful community of God. In short, the Christian church finds its locus wherever a decision is made to live by the fact that God the King is in charge of our common lives.

It follows, then, that the new community's form is not limited to our traditional denominational parish structures. Because a building stands on a corner and is given the name of a church does not mean that it necessarily houses the new community in Christ. Certainly no denominational organization is automatically synonymous with the new people of God. There may be ecclesiastical structures within our world which totally deny God's kingship.

But, as we have emphasized before, there are at least two essential characteristics that distinguish the church. First, it is a community of faithful believers and not just a group of individuals, for the simple reason that God wills it to be a community. Let no woman reject church membership in favor of an individualistic spiritualism! Second, at the center of the church's life there stands the Word of God. Only in that Word, incarnate in Christ, the church finds its revelation of the Lord. Only by trust in that Word, proclaimed and interpreted responsibly, can the church truly live as the new community of God. Insofar as both of these characteristics are found in our traditional church structures, those structures continue to express the true nature of God's new community. The church must always have some kind of a meeting point, where it comes together as a visible community and where it worships and learns together, in common, under the Word. But the point to remember is that the traditional structures, organizations, programs, and activities of the churches do not make up the church. The church is constituted by God's reign revealed in Christ and by our trusting response to it.

It seems to me, therefore, that it is not half so important to be busy in a church building as it is to be living the life of the church wherever we may find ourselves. God does not set aside a special sacred realm and demand that we confine ourselves to it. He does not ask that we all retreat to a monastery or journey to a missionary outpost. He does not ask that we all enter an ecclesiastical vocation. He does not even ask that we spend several days a week within our local church buildings. Rather, God's requirement of his "saints in Christ" is that we trust his kingship, *now, where we are.* And most of us are middle-class housewives, in normal American families. How then do we trust God's rule in the midst of such normality? What does it mean to be a member of the new community in Christ and an ordinary woman? We cannot answer these questions in the fullest possible detail. We can give some concrete examples of the direction their answers should take. Let us look first of all at God's lordship over marriage.

1.

The basic presupposition of all Christian marriage is the trust that God actively desires the particular union and that he has included it in his working and plan for his world.

Certainly throughout the Bible the community of marriage is affirmed. We are told in Genesis 1 that it was by a special intention and act, differing from every other creative act, that God made male and female in his image, blessed them, and commanded them to multiply (Gen. 1:27-28). In the more searching story of Genesis 2, God is pictured in thought: "It is not good that the man should be alone," he muses, after the creation of Adam, "I will make him a helper fit for him" (Gen. 2:18). Thus woman is made from the rib of man and brought to the man by God himself. And as soon as the man is given his wife, he shouts out in ecstatic joy: "This at last is bone of my bone and flesh of my flesh." "Therefore," the story continues, "a man leaves his father and his mother and cleaves to his wife, and they become one flesh" (Gen. 2:22-24)—all because marriage is a good and joyful gift of community which God has willed for us.

Throughout the Old Testament, this affirmation of marriage continues. The wife "like a fruitful vine" within the house and the children "like olive shoots" around the table: these are the gifts, the psalmist says, from God to his faithful follower (Ps. 128:3-4). To the author of Proverbs, a good wife "is far more precious than jewels" (Prov. 31:10).

> Her children rise up and call her blessed;
> her husband also, and he praises her:
> "Many women have done excellently,
> but you surpass them all" (Prov. 31:28-29).

Marriage, for the Old Testament writers, makes up an indispensable part of the goodness of the original creation (cf. Gen. 1:31). The disruption or the denial of marriage is, therefore, to some of the prophets, one of the strongest symbols of God's judgment [2] (Isa. 4:1; Jer. 16:1-13; Ezek. 24:15-27). And in the stories of Genesis, it is only after the Fall that polygamy enters the scene, as a sinful corruption of God's original good intention (Gen. 4:19).

The union of marriage furthermore serves the biblical writers as a symbol of the love of God, and frequently God's relations with his people are framed in the metaphors of marriage (Isa. 50:1; 54:4-8; 62:4-5; Ezek. 16; Hos. 2:19-20; Rev. 19:6-7). Indeed, the community of marriage is so good in the eyes of God that it becomes the earthly symbol of Christ's relation with his church

---

[2] Some German theologians have suggested that the large number of unmarried women in their country—the result of Germany's loss of her young men in World Wars I and II—serves God's purpose of reminding our age that we, too, stand under judgment.

(Eph. 5:21-33). As Christ is one with the body of his people, so husbands are to be one with their wives. And as Christ loves his church as himself, husbands are to love their mates. There is in the basic microcosmic community of marriage a mirror or fore-taste of God's universal community with his own. The marrriage of man and wife, in its goodness, can point to the kingdom of God (cf. Rev. 19:6-8).

It is not surprising, then, that the community of marriage is always pictured as a permanent relationship on this earth, and that its unity is carefully surrounded and guarded by the commandments of God himself. The seventh of the Ten Commandments uncompromisingly forbids adultery (Exod. 20:14; Deut. 5:18). Jesus affirms the oneness of man and wife and then specifically adds, "What therefore God has joined together, let not man put asunder" (Mark 10:2-12). Paul emphasizes that he is speaking for God when he forbids sexual immorality and divorce (I Cor. 7:10-11; I Thess. 4:1-8), just as earlier the prophet Malachi had voiced the Lord's hatred of such marital unfaithfulness and disruption (Mal. 2:13-16). To be sure, the Bible pictures the marriage covenant as terminated by death (Matt. 22:30; Rom. 7:2-3), the implication being that the limited community of marriage is fulfilled and perfected after death by the larger community of the kingdom. But while life is lived on this earth, the Bible sees marriage as commanded and protected by God. It is a form of community willed by the Lord and is given as a gift of his goodness.[3]

Within the marriage relationship, the Bible furthermore posits particular roles for man and wife. They are to form a union in which each complements and fulfills the other. We are all sometimes amused, very often frustrated, and occasionally heartbroken by the pattern of competition between male and female which

---

[3] This is not to say that the Bible does not make room for some who are called to remain single. Cf. Matt. 19:10-12; I Cor. 7.

has come to be called "the battle of the sexes" in our society. The common picture is of the dominant and embattled male, fighting to protect his masculinity and superiority from the encroachments of scheming females. Women in pants, women in business, "togetherness" and "mom-ism": these have become the symbols of the enemies of masculinity.

It is significant that in the biblical creation narrative, the "battle of the sexes" does not exist. It is only as the result of sin that woman is subjected to that humiliating domination by her mate (Gen. 3:16) from which she now apparently seeks so often to escape in modern America. In the original intention of God, however, as pictured in Genesis 2, man and wife are joined together for the purpose of completing each other. The woman is created from the body of her husband and finds wholeness only by returning to him (Gen. 2:22). The man is alone and unfulfilled in nature until given his corresponding partner (Gen. 2:20-23). Indeed, this is the meaning of the thought of God in Gen. 2:18: "I will make him a helper fit for (*corresponding to, kᵉnegdo*) him." The original Hebrew sense is of "complementing" or "making whole." Woman is given to man as his wife in order to fill out and complete his being. She is not intended as his subject, as his servant, or only as the mother of his children. The wife is intended by God to be the one who makes her husband whole, just as her union with her husband completes and fulfills her own being. Wife and husband do not necessarily do the same work. Their unity certainly is not limited merely to their sexual life. Rather, in the totality of life they complete and correspond to one another. Each is the necessary half to make the other half one.

Surely it is in this context that the statement of Paul should be read: "There is neither male nor female; for you are all one in Christ Jesus" (Gal. 3:28). By the redemption given us through trust in Jesus Christ, the primeval "battle of the sexes" is quieted and overcome. The original unity between man and wife, intended by God at creation, is restored to its possibility of wholeness and of mutual fulfillment.

These, then, form the basic presuppositions of the Christian marriage: God wills that the union exists. It stands under his blessing and protection. And the nature of the union is to be one in which man and wife make whole and complete each other. As such a union the Christian marriage finds an integral place in God's purpose. Indeed, it symbolizes and points forward to the final coming of God's kingdom, when God will enter into an eternal marriage with a renewed and faithful community encompassing all mankind. These are the presuppositions which we accept when we enter into a marriage in the church, that is, when we marry as members of God's new community.

I don't suppose anyone of us is *absolutely* certain before she weds that God desires that she take as her husband this particular man. Psychologists tell us that there are numerous persons with whom each of us could form a satisfactory union. And the rationalizations and passions of young love always make us sure that we have picked out God's chosen one for us. We can only look for common interests, common backgrounds, common values and beliefs with the man we marry, and try to temper our rationalizations and emotions with the light of reason. But our tendency after marriage, then, is to continue our rationalizations: if the relationship is a happy one we feel it was ordained by God from the foundation of the earth; if the relationship results in unhappiness, we become sure it was not intended by God—a view voiced to ministers quite frequently by young couples seeking divorce.

The point is that none of these rationalizations is synonymous with the Christian view of marriage. To enter into marriage in the church means to trust, from the time of the marriage onward, that God wills the union. It is this trust which the Christian marriage vows express:

I take thee to be my wedded husband, to have and to hold from this day forward, for better for worse, for richer for poorer, in sickness and in health, to love and to cherish, till death do us part, *according to God's holy ordinance;* and thereto I give thee my pledge.

By these vows we affirm our trust that God wills the marriage, that it is a relationship ordained and guarded by him, and that no matter what the circumstances, the relationship has a place in his purpose and is being used by him. Therefore we promise to preserve the marriage until its termination in death, and by our public statement of that promise, in the sight of God, we make it a binding covenant upon us. There is no question here of whether or not we have made a good choice. There is no conditional clause by which we may wait to see how it all works out. Trust in God's lordship over a Christian marriage has no "ifs" about it. It is to be a trust "from this day forward" that God the Lord wills the union and that he is actively accomplishing his purpose in it and through it. Christian marriage is the acceptance of a community between man and wife in the trust that the community is ordained and used by the Lord.

As we live out our married lives, therefore, we trust or we fail to trust every day by the things that we think and do in relationship to our husbands. We say that we believe God has willed our marriage. Why, then, do we upset the relationship God has willed by stamping out of the house in anger? Why do we disturb his community by quarreling over the breakfast table? Why do we belittle his will by belittling our husbands? These actions are not all just a matter of the psychological workings of a marriage. They concern, in Christian marriage, the affirmation or denial of trust.

135

And there are some glaring examples in modern American marriages where the quality of trust in God's lordship is lacking.

Let us take the example of the use of money within the home. We wives are working more outside of our homes and earning more wages than ever before. Psychologists and sociologists who have studied the phenomenon say we are doing so for a variety of reasons. But whatever our motivations involved, there comes a time for our wages to be spent, and the way we spend them can say a great deal about our trust in the lordship of God. So many of us are inclined to believe, after we have earned a little, that the fruit of our work is "my money" to be spent as "I" alone see fit. Suddenly we no longer believe ourselves involved in an unbreakable union which God has willed. We consider ourselves, with money in our purses, individuals with separate powers and desires. The husband, because it is the pattern of society, must give his earnings for all the family. But we working wives, we tend to feel, can use our earnings for ourselves. Thus we deny that God has bound us together in monetary affairs with a husband, and often that denial shakes the marriage God has willed to its very roots. Women divorce their husbands more easily these days because they have the financial independence to support themselves. And it is very often exactly that independence with which they have progressively destroyed God's willed community from the beginning.

This is not to argue that women should not work outside of their homes. It is not a repudiation of the many different equitable arrangements whereby the wife is given an "allowance" or "extras" to use for her needs and interests. Rather, it is to illustrate the fact that we affirm or deny the lordship of God over marriage in very concrete and specific ways. And often by selfishly claiming our money for ourselves we deny the community of husband and wife which God the Lord has willed. To trust that God desires our wedded relationship means to affirm that relationship by our actions. Our trust is acted out in the specific decisions of our everyday life.

The same reasoning can be applied to almost any area of marital life. To cite another example, we should ask ourselves about those careers we are pursuing outside of our homes. Do they indeed make whole our relationship with our husbands? Or are they pursued in a spirit of competition with him, in order that we, too, may win some independent recognition for ourselves? There is a great difference between following natural interests, which tend to enrich a marriage, and working to build a success and reputation in a field for ourselves.

Or consider our friendships. Every woman should be blessed with the comfort and companionship of female friends. But there is a point where interests or time shared with acquaintances or relatives can shut out all consideration for the husband God has given us.

In all of these areas—money, work, companionship, indeed in every decision, including the ones having to do with sex and the raising of our children—we have to ask ourselves if we are affirming the will of God by building up and making whole the marital community in which God has placed us. Or are we denying God's lordship and refusing to trust him, by asserting our independence and self-will over against our husbands? Those actions which are done selfishly for ourselves alone are a concrete denial of the fact that God has not intended us to live alone.

It is in this light, it seems to me, that the problem of divorce must be seen; for divorce is, in many cases, the final refusal to trust. The basic expectation in most American marriages has become one of "happiness." It is considered that a woman marries to make herself happy. Indeed, the right to be happy (which can mean almost anything!) has become in many of our homes *the* American right. And the whole success or failure of a union is judged on the basis of this right. If a wife does not find happiness with her husband, then she is considered to have the further right to divorce her mate and to go in search of one who will better fulfill her needs. In other words, no longer is the marital union, willed by God, the prime consideration. It has been superseded in importance by the individual's right to bliss. Divorces are thereby granted on the basis of "indignities" or "incompatibility"—terms which very often signify nothing more than selfishness. As one woman put it, "If my marriage weren't successful, I'd give it up in a minute." There is nothing in such a statement which indicates that God has willed her marriage or that he is using it in any way in his purpose.

The fact is that Christian trust holds that God the Lord has willed our marriage "for better for worse, for richer for poorer, in sickness and in health." Christian trust means to affirm God's will, even from the midst of unhappiness! We are all well aware of the fact that every marriage has its problems. The distinctively Christian affirmation we forget is that God also uses those problems! God wills and is at work in a marriage, even during its most hellish days. To cling to that fact is what it means to trust God's lordship over our relations with our husbands.

I do not believe the church can make any blanket rules about divorce. There are truly exceptional cases in which to refuse divorce would be a denial of the mercy of Christ and a literal consignment of an innocent sufferer to a living hell on earth. But as members of God's new community in Christ, we can refuse to substitute our own personal self-centered happiness for trust in the will of God. One of the most "happily" married men I ever knew once said to me, "There are times when a marriage is held together by nothing more than duty." By duty the speaker—a Christian professor—meant duty to his God, duty to live the life of the new people in Christ, duty to trust the Lord. Truly, such duty or trust is the foundationrock of a Christian relationship: "I take thee to be my wedded husband, . . . for better for worse, . . . till death do us part, according to God's holy ordinance."

2.

To live as members of the new community in Christ means not only to trust God's will as Lord. It further means to trust God's kingly forgiveness in Christ. This trust, too, is acted out in the details of our daily life.

As Christians, we are all aware of the proclamation that God has forgiven and accepted us in Jesus Christ. We examined this proclamation at some length in our earlier discussion. But again, we women often tend to limit the fact of forgiveness to the ecclesiastical realm. Forgiveness, for us, is something we receive in the Sunday morning worship service for all of the things we think we have done wrong during the week. Actually, however, it is God's forgiveness in Christ which sustains the whole of our existence. And while it is the task of the church to proclaim that forgiveness ever anew, it is also our task as "saints in Christ" to trust that forgiveness in every act we do.

You and I would bear a terrible weight of guilt in our homes without God's forgiveness of us. For not one of us can honestly say that we have always affirmed God's ordained community of marriage and of the family. There are times when our selfishness has sorely disrupted our relationships with our husbands. There are times when our tiredness or ignorance or prideful power has led us to be unjust and careless toward our children.

Indeed, in relation to our children our sins of omission and commission become glaring. What one of us has not disciplined her child because she, not the child, was cross? What one of us has not burdened her children with undue fears or anxieties? What one of

139

us has not imposed on her offspring her prides and prejudices? Truly the Bible is profoundly correct when it says that the children suffer for the sins of the parents.

But the worst is that so many of our sins against our children are so well-meaning and so unintentional. Somehow our love for our children is mixed up inseparably with our rebellions and fears and desires. And though we think we would die for our offspring, we cannot help warping them with our weakness. A woman becomes painfully aware of the mistakes she has made in her role as a mother. If she were called to account for all those mistakes, she would be placed under terrible condemnation.

The amazing truth is, however, that there is a grace which surrounds our lives, which constantly forgives our sinful errors and holds out the possibility of a new beginning. Every mother has had the experience of unjustly punishing a child, only to have that little one minutes later smother her with kisses. In a little child's love for us, despite our errors and injustices, we are time and again offered the experience of forgiveness, which makes it possible to go on. Our little children do not normally hold us accountable for our sins. Instead, they mediate a new beginning approximating the forgiveness of God.

During all of our lives we parents are recipients of such forgiving grace, for by God's merciful providence our children mature and prosper in spite of us. They bear the wounds of our sins and errors, to be sure. Sometimes, to all appearances, they are destroyed by those wounds. There can be no doubt that we parents bear an awful responsibility. Usually and miraculously, however, our children grow up to live full and wholesome lives, and our errors are overcome and healed by a power and intention beyond us. God guides and works with the lives of our children, in spite of our sins against them, and the fact that he does so constitutes a merciful forgiveness of us as erring parents.

If God did not so work through Jesus Christ, if he were not actively forgiving by his Word, we parents would be crushed by the weight of our guilt and regret and despair. But God does so work, and it is given us to trust that work of mercy. In all of our relations with our children we are asked to trust that God is at work in forgiveness. Indeed, even when we think we have completely ruined our child, even when we know we have been totally derelict in our duty, trust in the lordship of God means to trust that he forgives.

I shall never forget a former neighbor of mine who had an especially difficult time with her firstborn. The infant needed a special formula; it cried almost constantly day and night; the husband was often out of town and unsympathetic to the new mother's plight; her dishes stacked up higher and higher; her household routine became chaos. Finally, one morning as the weary mother walked the floor with her screaming infant, she said very bitterly, "I wish this baby would catch pneumonia and die!" Of course the baby did not die, and the mother finally mastered her new tasks, but her hostility toward her infant son has been shared by many a new parent. Many parents, in trying circumstances, literally hate their children. If we do not trust that there is forgiveness through Jesus Christ for that hate, we can be destroyed by the remembrance of it.

Actually because God has forgiven us through his Son, there is no circumstance where his act of mercy does not apply, and there is no failure which should drive the Christian to say, "I can never forgive myself." God has already forgiven us by the cross of Christ, and to trust in his lordship means to accept ourselves, too, as forgiven and acceptable. We pointed this out in Chapter II when we said that God gives us the power in Christ to continue our battle against our evils. We have to repent of those evils, to be sure. We have to want to make a new beginning. But we are not to be overcome by the wrong we have done in the past. We are not to condemn ourselves. We are not to be despairing. Rather, we are to trust that in Jesus Christ God gives us the possibility of a new beginning. For by the sacrifice of his Son on the cross, God has done just that.

Trust in God's forgiving lordship means not only that we are to accept ourselves. It further means that we are to accept the members of the community in which God has placed us, whether that be the community of our families or the wider, potentially universal, community of the church.

I once knew a young pastor who was shaken to his emotional roots by the unexpected divorce suit of his wife, but the reason for much of his difficulty became apparent when he produced his diary. It contained an account of all of the wrongs he had suffered at the hands of his wife! For five years he had recorded her mistakes, ineradicably impressing them in his memory as he wrote them down in ink. There was no doubt that his wife had done him some terrible injustices. From all appearances he was in truth married to a shrew. The difficulty was that he cast aside all possibility for the redemption of his marriage by his failure to forgive "seventy times seven" (Matt. 18:22). The historical fact he overlooked was that God in Jesus Christ had forgiven his wife, and to trust God's lordship meant that he must forgive her too—not once, not twice, but day after day, in every new quarrel and fresh difficulty.

You see, God the Lord has forgiven all those people with whom we so often get into difficulty—our mates, our parents, our friends, our assorted relatives and acquaintances. Some of them may be rather unpleasant people. Some of them undoubtedly do not deserve a shred of consideration. In God's eyes none of us do! But the fact is that the act has taken place. At the place called Golgotha the forgiveness has been wrought. And because of that fact God has declared all of those people acceptable in his eyes.

To trust God's lordship, therefore, means to accept God's decision. It means to act toward other people on the basis of God's acts toward them. It means to adopt his position wholeheartedly as our position. It means to take those people exactly as they are, forgiven and acceptable in our eyes, because they are forgiven and acceptable in God's. We cannot oppose our view of other people to God's view of them and still claim that we trust God to be the Lord of life.[4] If God is Lord, his is the final view. And in Jesus Christ he has declared that all are acceptable in his sight.

It seems to me that this is one of the reasons for the great thankfulness of the Christian. I do not praise my God because he has forgiven me alone. I praise him because he has forgiven all men. I praise him because as Lord he has wrested the judgment of my fellows out of my hands and replaced my blind ignorance and folly with his accepting mercy. No longer am I called upon to separate the "sheep" from the "goats." No longer have I the necessity of judging and discerning character, of futilely deciding on the basis of my prides and prejudices who is good and who is bad, of raising or lowering my guard against my neighbors according to the mores of the day. There are no in-group and out-group any longer. There is no one who is the social pariah on the block and whom I must therefore shun to be proper. There are no social blue book and black list to tell me with whom to be seen. There is only that "friend of publicans and sinners" through whom God has made all men acceptable. And because of him I now confront a whole world of acceptable people.

I am, in Jesus Christ, suddenly introduced into a community without barriers, a community in which status and stereotypes and

[4] This is simply another way of stating the well-known passage of I John 4:19-21: "We love, because he first loved us. If any one says, 'I love God,' and hates his brother, he is a liar; for he who does not love his brother whom he has seen, cannot love God whom he has not seen. And this commandment we have from him, that he who loves God should love his brother also."

143

pride and prejudice no longer have any meaning. It is a community in which all are made equal brothers by God. And thanks be to God in Jesus Christ, I too have been forgiven and set free in it to love!

This is what the Bible means when it says God has broken down the barriers between us (cf. Eph. 2:13-22). In Jesus Christ God has created the new reality of a community without dividing lines, because it is a community totally forgiven and acceptable in his sight. Without God's act of forgiveness in Christ such a community does not exist. But because Christ is real, the community is real, and it is experienced by those who trust God the Lord.

It is only in such trust that the church can possibly exist as the church, as the community brought together by God's forgiving act in Jesus Christ. Goodness knows we can never formulate our own membership lists! Were I to be given the responsibility to-morrow of drawing up the church's roll, there would be ever so many whom I, in my sin, would have to eliminate from the new community immediately: my dear friend who alternates between worship of nature and of herself, the confused soul around the corner who mixes Christianity and Bahai, the insecure and bitter woman who makes a habit of insulting her friends, the useless gossip who weekly tears apart the fabric of our common life, even the lonely and the weak who constantly ask and never give—all would have to be eliminated if mine were the judgment to make. But heading the list of those to be dropped, there would also have to stand your name—and mine. For we, too, by human judgment, do not deserve a place in the new life of God's community. I suppose this is what Jesus meant when he said, "Judge not, that you be not judged" (Matt. 7:1), for if the standard is our human measure, not one of us is acceptable. Only insofar as we let God be the judge, only as our measures give way to his mercy, only as we trust our assessment to his hands, do we all come to hear the verdict, "Acceptable and not guilty in Jesus Christ." It is through his Son that God establishes his new community. By trust in his mercy in Jesus Christ, we too join the company of God's new, forgiven people.

3.

Finally, to trust God's lordship in Jesus Christ means to see all things in the light of the kingdom. It means to cling fast to the fact, in every act, that God's is the final outcome.

There is no one who reminds me of this fact quite so much as do those women among my acquaintances who happen to be spinsters. By the superficial standards set up in our society, these unwed women are sometimes considered failures. As I pointed out in Chapter I, many consider that unmarried women have failed to achieve their proper role. They have, for one reason or another, failed to become wives and mothers. But my unwed friends make a different impression on me. They serve as a marvelous witness to me of the sovereignty of God. They remind me of the fact that ours is not the final judgment, and that it is God who will ultimately determine who has been a success or failure.

Furthermore, the Scriptures tell us that when God makes his judgment, he will not do so according to our commonly accepted values. Rather, he will turn our standards completely upside down. We reward the outstanding, the gifted, the self-reliant. But God gives his gift of eternal life to the meek and to the powerless. He does not offer the kingdom to the strong, the successful, the important people. Rather, its prize is inherited by the weak, the poor, the souls who are helpless in our world: "Blessed are the poor in spirit, for theirs is the kingdom of heaven. Blessed are those who mourn, for they shall be comforted. Blessed are the meek, for they shall inherit the earth" (Matt. 5:3-5).

> For I will leave in the midst of you
> a people humble and lowly. . . .
> They shall pasture and lie down,
> and none shall make them afraid (Zeph. 3:12*a*, 13*d*).

> The Spirit of the Lord is upon me,
> because he has annointed me to preach good news to
> the poor.
> He has sent me to proclaim release to the captives,
> and recovering of sight to the blind,
> to set at liberty those who are oppressed,
> to proclaim the acceptable year of the Lord (Luke 4:18-
> 19; cf. 7:22; Isa. 61:1-3).

In the same manner, it is not the powerfully rich Dives in the gospel who inherits the kingdom of Heaven. It is the powerless Lazarus, who has begged each day at the gate (Luke 16:19-31). God's final judgments in his kingdom upset the standards we have fixed in our society, and those whom we think to be unimportant failures may become first in the eyes of God.

The reason which the Scriptures give for this contradiction of our values is not that God desires to "even the score" by rewarding those who have had nothing out of life. Rather, God gives a place in his kingdom of life to the totally defenseless, because it is precisely the totally defenseless who can rely on nothing and no one besides God. It is the meek, the poor, the unimportant, the powerless who look to God for their lives and strength, and in such trustful reliance on God they fulfill all of the demands of faith. We are acceptable in the eyes of God, not because of our social status, but to the extent that we have a "broken spirit" and a "contrite heart" (Ps. 51:17). God will receive us into his eternal community only by our reliance on the forgiveness and new life he has made available in his Son. And if we would be members of his new community, we must be ever mindful of such facts.

We idolize power in modern America, on every level of our society: the power of money, the power of influence, the power of accomplishment and know-how. It is the woman who can charm, who can lead, who can influence, to whom we pay our respect, whether she impresses merely her neighbors or the whole of her community. But from the perspective of the kingdom of God, to be members of God's new community means to be willing to be powerless—powerless in matters of money and status, powerless even in matters of religion. It means to rely on no other helper besides God the Lord to give us abundant life.

This is not to consign the Christian woman to a drab and uninteresting existence. Heaven deliver us from the black-dressed, joyless dowdy-ism of the rigid pietist! One can be as enslaved to pietism as to any other kind of selfishness, and slavery in any form—except to Christ—is a denial of the joyful freedom which God has given to his children. The Christian woman can be tastefully dressed and run a well-furnished house. If she is a good cook or a polished hostess or an accomplished conversationalist, she will delight all who know her. But as a "saint in Christ" she will also have to check carefully on her own motives and activities.

There is a difference between enjoying God's good gifts in life and using them for social climbing. There is a difference between the appreciation of beauty and the employment of it to enhance one's prestige. There is a difference between utilizing talents and controlling other people with them. There is a difference between glorifying oneself and glorifying God the Lord. If we use the gifts God has given us to increase our own prestige and power, we will in the end be faced with the uncomfortable fact that to God alone belong the power and the glory. God's judgments as to who is important are different from ours. And in the kingdom he will ask

147

us only one question: Have we trusted him? (cf. Luke 18:8). The meek, the faithful, the poor in spirit, the powerless will be able to answer, "Yes, Lord."

It takes a mighty wrestling in ourselves to give up our strivings for power. It means giving up our desire for control over other people's lives. It means being willing to trust the whole outcome to the hands of the living Lord. And we may very well have to know him much better through his Word before we are willing to do that. But trust in the Lord is never misplaced, and it is never in vain.

Indeed, to go further, it is trust in our King which makes abundant life possible today. We modern women are not, like our counterparts of one hundred years ago, confined and sheltered in our homes. While we pursue the normal tasks of housewife and mother, the whole world pushes itself into our attention. As my nine-year-old leaves for school, he calls back, "Come get me if we have an air raid." And the adolescent son of a neighbor confesses that he plans to be an architect, "If we haven't been blown up by then." International crises are a part of normal conversation in the kitchen these days, and we ordinary housewives know ourselves surrounded by threats of chaos and destruction on every side.

If we truly trust God's lordship, however, if we cling to the fact that his kingdom comes, even the insane world we live in is seen in a context of sanity. We so often anxiously believe that the entire future is in our hands. We are told that our life or death hangs in the nuclear balance of power, that the welfare of our children depends on how we deal with population explosions and mental illnesses, that we can chart the course of the world by how we administer foreign aid in Asia or in Africa. As a series of advertisements put it in a popular magazine, "Our destiny is in our hands." Somehow we are anxiously uncertain that we can handle the responsibility.

The truth is that because of Jesus Christ our destiny is *not* in our hands, and that even if we blow up the world, the final decision will not have been made. The destiny, the eternal life, the goal of our living, all lie in the hands of God. And for all of our uses and misuses of our power, his is the final outcome. God's kingdom will come on his earth (cf. Rev. 21-22), even as it is in heaven, and to live the life of the new community means to live, without fear, by that fact.

If we can commit all things into the hands of our God, if through knowledge of his Word made flesh we gradually come to rely on him, if even in the middle of suffering and evil we begin to see God at work, then we shall indeed be granted a real peace which the world can neither give nor take away. We shall find a joy and certainty given only to the saints in Christ. For these are based on trust and the unshakable knowledge that God reigns as King and Lord.

IN QUIETNESS AND TRUST

> In returning and rest you shall be saved,
> in quietness and in trust shall be your strength (Isa. 30:15).

When Isaiah spoke these words from God, Israel was beset on every side. Her ten northern tribes had disappeared from history into exile. Her southern territory had been laid waste by the pillaging troops of the Assyrian Empire. Her political and judicial life was infested with drunkards and grafters. Her religious and family practices were ostentatious sham. But in the midst of the confusion, Isaiah saw a hand stretched out—the hand of the Almighty King and Holy One of Israel. It was the same hand of the same King that had redeemed the prophet himself (Isa. 6:1-7), and Isaiah knew that in its grasp lay might and love and life. Thus the prophet bid his people grasp God's hand and trust his strength and love, for in her quiet trust in God lay Israel's salvation.

The same hand of the same God is stretched out to us today. In the good news of Jesus Christ, the Lord offers to us new life. As I have tried to show in this little book, it is a life of great freedom— freedom from enslaving stereotypes and meaningless idolatries and traditional strifes. It is a life of freedom from fear and despair and guilt.

At the same time, the new life God offers us is a life of re- sponsibility—responsibility to the Lord in the context of a com- munity, responsibility to be a person who has been made for a purpose by the Creator, responsibility to make decisions for or against God's will.

Still more, the new life offered us in Jesus Christ is a life of meaning. It sees that the endless cycle of nature is going somewhere, under God. It finds in the midst of suffering and evil the purpose of a loving Lord. It sanctifies the routine of daily life with the presence of the King of kings and demands that the secular also be understood as the realm of his activity.

Finally, the new life God holds out to us is a life of confidence, because it knows that God is present and at work to bring in his eternal kingdom.

We can participate in this new life offered us, by trust in Jesus Christ, by seeing in him the certain revelation of God's rule over the earth. But that revelation cannot be granted us as mere dogma or on the basis of hearsay. It is a knowledge which can come to us only through our own meeting with the Word of God. No second- hand religious opinion is sufficient to convey it to us. No emotional "spiritual" experience or theory will manifest its truth. No well- meaning human illogicality, no matter how "religious," will ever reveal the lordship of God as it has been made known in Jesus Christ. That lordship has been revealed only in the history to

151

which the Bible gives witness. And we have to make that history our own before we can recognize our Lord. We have to begin to *understand* God's Word before we can trust him. We have to come to *know* whom it is we have believed.

It seems to me that such transforming theological knowledge and understanding, gained from the Bible, are worth the effort they may cost us. For out of them come that quietness and trust that lead to life, to strength, to salvation.

SUGGESTED HELPS
FOR BIBLE STUDY

Achtemeier, Paul J. and Elizabeth. *The Old Testament Roots of Our Faith*. Nashville: Abingdon Press, 1962.

Anderson, B. W. *Understanding the Old Testament*. New York: Prentice-Hall, Inc., 1957.

—— *The Unfolding Drama of the Bible*. New York: Association Press, 1957.

Blair, Ed. P. *The Bible and You: A Guide for Reading the Bible in the Revised Standard Version*. Nashville: Abingdon Press, 1953.

Bright, John. *A History of Israel*. Philadelphia: The Westminster Press, 1959.

—— *The Kingdom of God*. Nashville: Abingdon Press, 1953.

Good, E. M., editor. *Westminster Guides to the Bible*. 9 vols. Philadelphia: The Westminster Press, 1959-62.

Hunter, A. M. *Introducing New Testament Theology*. Philadelphia: The Westminster Press, 1958.

The Interpreter's Bible. 12 vols. Nashville: Abingdon Press, 1951-57.

The Interpreter's Dictionary of the Bible. 4 vols. Nashville: Abingdon Press, 1962.

Kelly, B. H., editor. *The Layman's Bible Commentary*. 25 vols. Richmond: John Knox Press, 1960-64.

Rowley, H. H. and Black, M., editors. *Peake's Commentary on the Bible*. Revised edition; New York: Thomas Nelson & Sons, 1962.

Wright, G. E. and Filson, F. V., editors. *The Westminster Historical Atlas to the Bible*. Revised edition; Philadelphia: The Westminster Press, 1956.

INDEX OF BIBLICAL REFERENCES

157